LISTEN
TO THE WIND
SPEAK FROM THE HEART

ROGER THUNDERHANDS GILBERT

DIVINE
ARTS

Published by DIVINE ARTS
DivineArtsMedia.com

An imprint of Michael Wiese Productions
12400 Ventura Blvd. #1111
Studio City, CA 91604
(818) 379-8799, (818) 986-3408 (FAX)

Cover Design: Johnny Ink. www.johnnyink.com
Cover Painting: Tom Perkinson, Exposures International Gallery
Book Layout: William Morosi
Copyeditor: Matt Barber
Printed by McNaughton & Gunn, Inc., Saline, Michigan

Manufactured in the United States of America

Library of Congress Cataloging-in-Publication Data

Gilbert, Roger Thunderhands, 1946-
 Listen to the Wind Speak from the Heart / Roger Thunderhands Gilbert.
    p. cm.
 ISBN 978-1-61125-011-4
 1. Indians of North America--Religion. 2. Indian philosophy--North America. 3. Spiritual life--North America.
I. Title.
 E98.R3G54 2012
 299.7--dc23

                              2012017724

Printed on Recycled Stock

"*Listen to Wind Speak from the Heart* is a heart-filled book of wisdom, storytelling, prayers, and soul-provoking messages. Roger Thunderhands Gilbert clearly is messenger-as-guide, supporter and elder, as he walks with us through the pages of our own spiritual path. A remarkable easy-reading book for all paths of life. I found the words inspiring and food for my soul. Many blessings on this endeavor brother. AHO!!!"

— Cuauhtli Cihuatl Mexhika Eagle Woman

"Knowing Thunderhands has been akin to knowing the difference between wisdom and passion, and how both can be indivisible in the essence of one man. Thunder is a master healer. He asks that you not follow him, just hear him, and listen, see him, and attend. I'm suggesting that you do come in for awhile and partake in Thunder's banquet fit for a Taoist feast! Feel free to travel with Thunder, a spiritual healer, my friend, and a Gift of Grace. My gratitude to him is like a clear river ever-evolving to become an ocean."

— Ilene "Arrow" Sandman, MA, Professor of Humanities

"Beginning with one man's thirst for the teachings of the Elders, *Listen to the Wind Speak from the Heart* touches the journey of humanity, longing to give us the tools to make tomorrow more meaningful than today. Thunderhands' commentary gives light and hope at the core of each message, transcending what can be the silent and passive response to life, to transformative and vibrant existence. You only need to walk the path that is offered to you. Through his writings, we learn of love and life, responsibility to the self, the planet, and the people. The human spirit cannot be forever silent, and Thunderhands shares what the generations have known for all time—the wisdom of those who walked before us, who walk with us, and for those who will come after us. This is an important read for those interested in Native American wisdom and reason, critical to a future of inner peace and our impact upon each other."

— Billie K. Fidlin, President, Whisper n Thunder Inc.

Contents

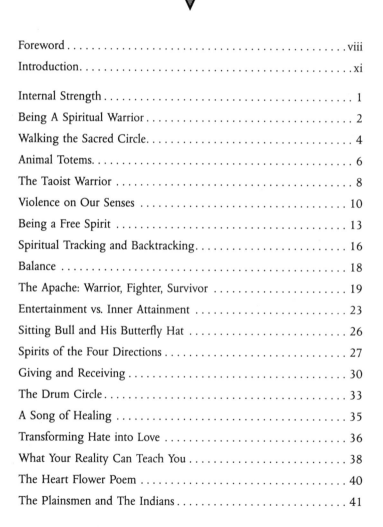

Foreword

▼

WHEN I FIRST SAW that Thunderhands described himself as a Native American Taoist, I was very curious to see the ways in which this was expressed.

Imagine sitting around a campfire in a timeless setting, listening to a wise elder, a sage, an ancient soul speak wisdom so deep that each short tale could be life-changing. Imagine that these stories, told in a casual, conversational campfire tone, were each a key to another door of enlightenment. Imagine the shock some would feel when the realization finally came to them that the truth is not only much simpler than we try to make it, but that it is also much easier to access than society has indoctrinated us to believe.

This is what Thunder does in *Listen to the Wind Speak from the Heart*. He listens to the wind, the inner/higher spirit in himself and in all things. He speaks from the heart, passing on the wisdom of the spirit in plain, understandable, passionate language. In doing this he models an example to each person who reads his thoughts, in the hope that some will find the keys within and open new doors to their own paths of enlightenment. His eclectic spirituality and strong extensive knowledge combine to create an environment where each person can take away something uniquely meaningful, and even life changing, from his writings. When you read his words, you can't help but feel the power in the lessons of life that bring wisdom and knowing. You can't help but feel the strength of the breath of spirit that speaks from his heart.

In many of the sections of the book Thunder's Native American heritage is strongly expressed in an inclusive and instructive manner, inviting all who read to join in. In other sections the Taoist, and more, are evident. What you won't find is conflict. Thunder's integration of eclectic spirituality, world view, spiritual links to Mother Earth, and all he discusses blend in a perfect mix that leaves no agitation, no confusion, no conflict. If one listens with an open heart to each section there is a very whole and uplifting feeling left within that heart. That is not to say that Thunder doesn't speak out with strong opinions and passion; he certainly does. But he has a way of bringing it all back around to the oneness of life and helping empower the reader towards balance and enlightenment.

He speaks of the Earth changes, and the spiritual meaning behind them, as well as the obvious physical causes. He speaks of the Mayan prophecies, and even of ancient star ancestors. He speaks of recent political events and protest movements, of recent upheavals in governments, and of how technology has linked the countries of the world so intricately that when massive changes come to one they will come to all. He talks of the food crisis that will arise with massive earth and economic changes. Yet, with all of this talk of decline and tragedy, he gives a message of hope. He explains in a variety of ways how all life is energy and that we are all one. He gives the reader tools to access this energy and to open his or her heart to a higher vibration, to learn to listen to the wind and to speak from the heart.

One of the most unique things about this book, in terms of accessibility, is that it is written in very short "campfire stories." It can literally be opened at any page, and within a page or two there will be a new "story" to read that is complete in itself, requiring no pre-reading or preparation. Each one is something to consider in itself. A reader could use each section as a thought to ponder for a day or a lifetime. Re-reading often brings even deeper meaning each time. That is the beauty of the layers of wisdom that are contained in these easy-to-digest segments.

The glossary is also very helpful because it allows an interested reader to learn more about many terms used in the book.

This is a compact book which illustrates perfectly the phrase, "Good things come in small packages." In *Listen to the Wind Speak from the Heart*, in Thunder's second book *Emergence*, and in listening to him channel the "holy wind" with his flute, there are messages of deep wisdom to be heard. Take this opportunity to sit around the campfire with Thunderhands and re-acquaint yourself with your higher self. It will stimulate your thinking and feeling, if nothing else, and you may find it will open doors to a whole way of thinking.

Carol Dixon, M Ed.
Educator, Editor, Poet
Author of:
Elemental Expression
From the Ashes
Co-author of *Symphony of Shadows*

Introduction

▼

GIVEN THE WORLD WE LIVE IN, with its uncertainties and changes, it sure doesn't hurt to have a few signposts along the way to guide us on our journey. The times we live in can be frustrating at the least, and terrifying at the most. My experiences in life have been trial-some at times and have bordered on outright survival. That's not to say there haven't been some very enlightening and enjoyable moments as well. But with each trial in my life came a learning experience that contributed to a cache of wisdom, if you will. And when times get tough it's always nice to know that you can listen to the wind. The term "listening to the wind" is from the Native American tradition, as is "speaking from the heart," or the "one eye of the heart" (Chante Ishta). My view of listening to the wind is listening to what nature, the universe, and your higher self is telling you, or maybe telling you to pass on to others. Speaking from the heart is conveying the messages you get from listening to the wind. It can also mean speaking straight and not with a forked tongue. There isn't much I want to say concerning this book because I don't want the reader to have any preconceived notions. I would rather you read it and take from it what serves you. Needless to say, I don't consider this a self-help book, but more of a "Spirit Help" book of counsel, or thoughts for consideration.

You travel the road of life and you write about things, and maybe these things will strike a chord with others. I leave it to Great Spirit as to whether or not this is meaningful for you. My intention is that some kind of healing will take place from the thoughts that I am offering. I believe in the old ways where a counsel of elders would sit around a campfire and speak their thoughts. I think if you take it in that spirit, this body of knowledge and tradition will be very appealing, healing, and calming on many levels. I would like to think that this is the kind of book that is timeless, and one you can come back to many times for answers. That was my inspiration. Look at it as a good friend with counsel for you on your journey along the path. There is a table of contents for reference, or just open the book anytime to any page or read in any order. I have included an extensive glossary at the back of the book for any terms you may not be familiar with, and I see it as an education in itself; so please don't hesitate to use it. This is my gift to you, from my heart to yours.

Mitakuye Oyasin (all my relations)
Thunderhands

DEDICATED TO MY SON AARON AND MY GRANDSON MILES.

Internal Strength

▼

IT'S ALL ABOUT INTERNAL STRENGTH, honor, and true humility, not if you win or lose, live or die, etc. It's how you live your life; i.e., not worrying about it, and not considering so much about right and wrong on the outside, or what someone else is doing that may be right or wrong. Strengthen the inner; refuse to do battle with the opponents within and without, so to speak. Refuse to confront the oncoming thrust of the sword—better to step aside and watch it miss its mark. Or better yet, take no thought on it. Hold no malice or anger for anything. Keep working on that inner light or the superior self, because that serves the better good. Work towards peace and harmony within and it will be reflected without. Sometimes you can win a battle, but that doesn't mean you win the war. Peace and harmony within brings good fortune for all concerned. It's about motive; we bring sorrow on ourselves and others by not being true to our higher self or good. It's like practicing the martial arts for glory and ego or practicing it to strengthen mind, body, and spirit, and to build character and humility. It's not about winning, even though you know you can. No matter what might face us, whether it be loneliness, relationships, or any kind of hardship, if we have that internal strength and walk with the sage, everything will be OK. As within so without. These words are easier to say than put into practice. And I guess that should be our goal; maybe we can't be perfect but we can work towards an ideal. Sometimes it does take a change in attitude or some event to cause a turning point in our lives.

Being A Spiritual Warrior

▼

BEING A SPIRITUAL WARRIOR is fighting battles that try to entrap you in the emotional games of this so-called reality. Most adults have scars and wounds on their souls after being in the matrix of Maya, or the illusion of this world. The spiritual reality of this battle is about healing and protecting. Healing what others have inflicted upon you, and what you perceive that you have done to others; and by warding off dark energy that comes in different forms in this seemingly never-ending drama called the third dimension.

Spiritual warriors study the martial arts and meditation techniques to prepare them to wield the sword of the spirit. They walk with one foot in the spirit world and one foot in the illusory reality. They take back and strengthen their personal power until it is strong, stable, and in balance. The fire of their spirit is strong, so they can balance others that they meet, while warding off their negativity and dark energy. It is about not believing everything you hear or have been indoctrinated with, since most of it was to serve others' purposes and most times consisted of lies or half truths, at best. Some people think what they have been indoctrinated with is good for you, too, and so they brainwash you from birth. Spiritual warriors find their own way by returning to the real truth, or the source. This source will empower them to do battle in a unique way, using spiritual weaponry.

It's all about energy, and duality. The spiritual warrior within you removes that which is blocking your way and the obstacles in your path. This can include such things as addiction, attachment to the lower physical realm, and dis-ease of body, mind, and spirit. This can be outside yourself in the form of people who need to be cured, and others who need to be eliminated from your life. If they have a fossilized mentality and belief system filled with hate, let spirit guide you to release them from your presence and to protect the ones you know who could be affected by this entity. The spiritual warrior has a type of vision that sees beyond the apparent form or illusion and cuts through the veil. The spiritual warrior has learned control and how to energy-shift and deal with any situation. The spiritual warrior is a soldier of the cosmos and universal mind which directs him to do battle by healing, and peaceful methods, while still having the power of a warrior. Being a spiritual warrior is learning the "sword of no sword" and "Mushin," which are the techniques of emptying the mind so spirit can work through him. It is the highest calling, because a warrior is a healer in the greatest sense of the word. It's a fine line that they walk and requires seeing with the third eye and feeling with extra senses. With warrior-ship comes the blessings of the spirit and the curse or responsibility of knowing and feeling things for which many have no clue. This includes empathy and feelings you pick up on and have to deal with while keeping yourself protected and centered. Does this calling sound hard? It becomes easier the more you let yourself be directed from above. As above so below. Everyone has the potential to train and be a spiritual warrior; do you hear the calling? I hope so; we need you. If you're not part of the solution, you've become part of the problem.

Walking the
Sacred Circle

▼

SOMETIMES WE THINK THAT as "human beings" we need to go to others for something that Mother Earth and Grandfather Sky have in abundance. We may think we want a companion and help-mate to give us love, support, and validation. That is OK and is a good thing. But do we try to hook up with people who are not walking our path just to have somebody, anybody? I suggest that the marvels of Mother Earth and her energy can supply me with an abundance of love, joy, and nurturing until the "Earth Woman" I want shows up. Where is there more feminine energy than in Unci, Maka, Grandmother Earth? And where can you get more elder energy, or strong counsel, than from Tunkashila, Grandfather Sky? Take a walk in the trees, lose yourself, and connect with the spirit that moves in all things. The trees, rocks, grass, and earth heal you with their auras. All of the plants, animals, and rocks (Inyan) have their own energy field; are you aware of that? Do you feel it? Do you let it mix with your aura? Do you let the wind blow the darkness from your soul? Do you listen to and ride on the wind, like brother Hawk, Crow, and Eagle? These are not just words, Mita Kola! The animals do a dance for you. In the sky it's the winged ones; on the ground it is the crit-ters, the four-legged ones. They will never lie to you, judge you, or send you dark energy. They will heal you with their antics and make you smile. The garden path they lead you down is the real one, the Red Road. They will never double-cross you or think that you are crazy! Their friendship is a given and only requires our acceptance. Don't turn your back on it, because life here is too short. Yes there are people around us too, and they need to be healed; and I love the two-legged ones, also. But when you give your love it is like trusting that they won't use what is given to them to hurt you. Protection is needed when healing and loving. Not all appreciate the wise counsel and love given. You will know by their actions, deeds, and words. You will also know by their dealings, and the people they surround themselves with. Are they centered and balanced? It's about love, not confusion. The critters are centered and balanced all the time, because they walk in "the sacred circle."

Animal Totems

DO YOU KNOW YOUR ANIMAL TOTEM? If you want to enhance your relationship with Great Spirit, the spirit that moves in all things, it might be a good idea to identify your totem. The further we get away from nature and our past connection with our shamanistic origins, the less we feel our connection. This is a sad loss for many reasons. Our totem can give us the power we need to overcome obstacles presented to us in this journey we call life. Anyone who owns a domestic animal will testify to the healing properties and love that they can impart to us. What animals do you identify with, dream about, or see on a regular basis? This could well be your totem. Each animal has a gift for you, so it would be beneficial to study the habits and spiritual properties of your totem or any animal or beast in the natural realm.

Spirit will appear, talk to, and guide you on your path through various animals. Go to the park, forest, or natural area and make note of the four-legged or winged ones that come into your view. Even a lizard on a rock is speaking to you. You can talk to them in a soft, kind voice and they will respond with a healing or direction for you to take. Meditate and ask that your totem come to you. Ask Great Spirit to reveal them to you. You can have more than one totem— one of the sky and one of the earth, or more than one of each, and one to help you in any circumstance in life. I was once doing a meditation and my feet got cold. Much to my amazement a bear appeared and lay in a fetal position around my feet, sending warm energy and love through my whole body.

I immediately realized that this was a totem animal that had been present in my life before, and as I opened my eyes I glanced at the Zuni bear fetish on my shelf that I had not been paying attention to. That night I put it next to my bed and thanked Great Spirit for reawakening my relationship with this powerful, yet loving, animal.

The Taoist Warrior

THE TAOIST WARRIOR SPEAKS only to guide. The Taoist warrior prefers silence because his guidance often falls on deaf ears, and so he leads by example. The Taoist warrior realizes "The Sword of No Sword." The Taoist warrior cares not for the mundane and trivial of which most of the world is comprised, excepting nature.

The Taoist warrior realizes that concepts of right and wrong are just that—concepts. The Taoist warrior cuts to the core without touching the bone. The Taoist warrior is not so concerned with morality and right or wrong, because one man's right is another man's wrong, and one man's morality is another man's immorality.

The Taoist warrior realizes that the past and future are a foggy mist that can't be grasped. The Taoist warrior realizes that all wars and enemies are generated from within. The Taoist warrior answers to no one, but walks with the Tao, which doesn't require answers, judging, or assigning blame. The Taoist warrior realizes that guilt, fear, and anger are a figments of the mind generated by earthly concepts and conditioning.

The Taoist warrior prefers nature and living alone. The Taoist warrior is a spiritual warrior and a spiritual man or woman. The Taoist warrior is perfect in that he is not perfect according to the ways of the world. The Taoist warrior is a traveler and wanderer, within and without. The Taoist warrior is often mistaken for having a cold heart, because he realizes detachment is true compassion for self and others.

The Taoist warrior is a calling few can comprehend, for how can the Tao be comprehended? The Taoist warrior doesn't comprehend; the Taoist warrior just is. The Taoist warrior realizes that he doesn't know, and that not knowing is the way of realization. The Taoist warrior can seem like a contradiction to others, for all things change and he flows with the change. This is called walking with the Tao!

Violence on Our Senses

THE CULTURE WE LIVE IN, the governments, and the social structure as a whole are committing violence against our senses. It is perpetuated by greed. We live in a reality that has departed from right thinking and that is out of balance.

Our sense of hearing is bombarded daily by alarming sounds. Loud machine noises abound everywhere in the sky and on earth. The sirens wail, the din of the freeway noise is continuous, and the media blares on and on about the most sensational, graphic situations on the planet. Loud boom-boxes in cars cruise by while garbage dumpsters are smashed violently against the ground. It is hard to hear the birds singing, the water in the streams flowing, and the wind blowing through the trees. It is hard to hear the summer rains and thunder.

Our sense of smell is accosted by the noxious fumes and pollution produced by gas-burning vehicles, power plants, and industry. It is difficult to stop and smell the roses or lilacs and newly mown fields. Our senses of touch and feeling are being restricted by the concrete and asphalt poured over Mother Earth, so that we cannot feel the grass between our toes and walk barefooted as nature intended. The heat rises from the concrete structures, causing a rise in temperature and preventing the breeze from blowing on our skin.

Our sense of taste is being dulled by processed foods and that quick snack at the local fast-food joint. Food doesn't taste like it used to. Our sense of sight is sickened at the rape of Mother Earth. Trees are hacked down, and bushes are trimmed to cubicle forms to fit in with the square mentality and the box-like structures we live in. No more circles and circles of life. Parks are turned into parking lots. Animals are shot and taken down because of their confusion on the intrusion.

And finally our sense of responsibility, fairness, and freedom are being dulled by the patriarchal system of greed, false power, and pride. The current mentality is to grab all you can while you can. The nature of man is no Nature at all.

So as a result we begin to shut down our senses. We narrow our view so as not to see. We dim our senses of smelling, feeling, and tasting because we don't like what we are being subjected to. We long for nature and times past from our ancestral memory. We pray for a place of silence in nature where we can gather our thoughts and return to some kind of normalcy. We ache to get off the treadmill of forced labor and slavery just to exist, and get back to oneness with Mother Earth as hunters and gatherers.

What can we do? What is the way out? Start by taking responsibility for your actions. Think coherently. It's hard because of the dulling of our sense of fairness to ourselves and others. Don't accept the status quo, and gently nudge yourself into another way of living. Start by turning off the TV and media brainwashing machine. If you can't find nature, start by having a small Zen fountain in your home with the running water. Or buy a CD with the sounds of running water and nature. Slow the heck down. Grow a garden in your house or on your balcony. Listen to soft music like the soothing sounds of Native American flute! Buy a bicycle and take some rides to nature, or the closest thing to it you can find. Make your thoughts prayers by envisioning what you want instead of what you don't want.

Alter your environment as much as you can and encourage others to do so. Start a community garden. Don't be an activist, but act-as-if! Heal your dulled senses slowly by treating them with love. Take relaxing showers and baths, explore aromatherapy, burn sage. Despite the forces around us, try to nurture your senses and bring them back. If you can get to a park, do some communing with nature. Nature heals, so become one with it. Follow animal tracks; notice the plants, shrubs and flowers around you. Learn which plants are edible and medicinal. Talk to nature, trees, animals, and everything else that is real. Feel the spirit that flows in all things. Don't be a victim; be a spiritual warrior and survivor. Project good imagery in your thoughts. Hey folks, this is beyond voting for your favorite guy or gal because you think they will do something for you. This is a spiritual thing, so heal your senses, regain your power, and project it. Thoughts are strong things; they create and form the world.

Being a Free Spirit

▼

I HAVE OFTEN BEEN ACCUSED OF, and have declared myself as being, a "Free Spirit." This can be a blessing or a curse, depending on how you look at it. The dictionary defines "free spirit" as the following: noun; a person with a highly individual or unique attitude, lifestyle, or imagination; nonconformist.

That being said, let me try to expound on what being a free spirit means to me, and/or how others view it. First, people who are free spirits may have at one time been oppressed or beaten down and vow never to be controlled again. Free spirits may listen and learn from masters, but as Jet Li put it in the movie *War*, "I have not betrayed my master, because I have no master." The only master they have is the highest one, the flow of life, the universe or the Tao, because it puts no demands on them and is non-judgmental, and therefore allows them to be their own master. This means there is no belief in an angry, unmerciful type God or entity ready to hail down fire and brimstone. Their concept is more of a higher power or creative force, free of codes of morality shaped by religious institutions.

Creative people are usually free spirits, and again, may be people who have been oppressed in the past. You can't trick a free spirit through manipulation, drama, or any other means. Since they are free; they see through the bullshit. Sometimes they have studied every means of manipulation you can imagine, including hypnotherapy, religion, and other forms of control like drama from certain relationships, just so they can avoid it. Now, being a free spirit has certain issues that must be recognized. First and foremost is the accusation that they are selfish and care for no one but themselves, and that they are cold. Nothing could be further from the truth. Being a free spirit doesn't mean you don't have compassion for other people's problems or suffering. As a matter of fact, you see these things quite clearly, but prefer non-attachment. How much better it is to help others from that perspective than to get involved in the drama? Being a free spirit means seeing the bigger picture and helping from that viewpoint.

Being a free spirit means that at times you find it to the benefit of all concerned to just walk away or to say no. In the martial arts this is called "The Sword of No Sword." Saying no is OK! It's a good thing sometimes. People get mad at free spirits when they walk away or say no, because they no longer have control. There are a lot of control issues going around these days. The government wants to control, religion wants to control, your mate, lover, family and so-called friends may want to control; and most times this is done, supposedly, for your own good. Free spirits realize this isn't always true. They usually see the ulterior motives. They listen, evaluate, and make a decision.

Sometimes being a free spirit allows you to see where other people are in bondage to a way of thinking and these others may prompt you to try to free them in some way. This is the hardest thing of all to a free spirit. Sometimes you are almost willing to sacrifice your freedom to help them, but when push comes to shove, if your help or words fall on deaf ears, there is nothing you can do except withdraw to keep your own free spirit intact. This doesn't mean you don't love them; in a sense it means you do. You finally realize they must walk their own path to "free spirit" status.

Spiritual Tracking
and Backtracking

▼

I HAVE BEEN GOING OVER Tom Brown Jr.'s books lately on tracking. On this read I am seeing applications at a spiritual level. One of the messages that is coming through to me is backtracking, or looking at what kind of "life tracks" you have left prior to this moment in time. By analyzing your tracks you can see how you have been walking the path up to this point. When you look at your own track you can see subtleties that can give you clues to the questions that might be cropping up in your life now. Do you feel unbalanced, or maybe indecisive as to the path you're on, or how to walk that path?

When a good tracker looks at someone's tracks he sees things no one else sees. He might look at a footprint and notice a slightly deeper furrow on one side, indicating things such as balance when walking, or maybe that the person or animal was lame and favored one foot. If you're a really good tracker you can determine how much change is in the guy's pockets. So look at your past tracks in the form of attitudes, missteps, and things that you might have done that brought you to now. Maybe you strayed down a wrong path and suffered a fall or had to correct course. Maybe you fell a couple of times and didn't learn the right way of walking so as not to fall again. Do you keep stubbing your toe because you refuse to walk softly? There is no sense in walking a walk that doesn't work for us.

By looking at the tracks in our life as a continuum, we can better determine the outcome, or even change it. We can make adjustments to our stride, or maybe walk like a cat instead of an elephant. Maybe we can become more aware of our surroundings, and even our beliefs. Do we believe that there is a monster just around the corner and walk in fear, or are we fearless because we know how to handle monsters from past experience? Good trackers are prepared for any contingency, so that whatever happens can be dealt with in the proper manner.

Be a spiritual tracker as well as a physical one. Study tracking and the ways of nature and apply what you learn to your life on a spiritual level. We can even watch the animals and their tracks and habits, learning from and applying them in our lives. Being in tune with nature and how it affects our nature will put us in oneness with the cosmos and our universal mind. If we get lost in a forest we can always backtrack to find our way out! May your path be filled with joy and wonderment as you traverse the road of life leading to the gateway of the next dimension.

Balance

BALANCE IS ABOUT RECOGNIZING and knowing intimately the natural forces and energies that flow within and without, and accepting them all equally and with love. When we accept all that is within and love it, all that is without mirrors this acceptance and love. Make something bad within and you are being harsh and judgmental on that part of yourself. Then when you see the reflection of this same thing on the outside, you are judgmental with that. It is all one. When you know and accept yourself, you become an embodiment of the universe and the natural order. Then things begin to flow for you and not against you. It's all about energy. The universe doesn't judge.

The Apache: Warrior, Fighter, Survivor

$\blacktriangledown$

THE APACHE WAS ONE of the most interesting tribes, in my opinion. I highly respect them for many reasons. The Apache people certainly lived in harmony with their environment. The desert region they lived in was harsh and unforgiving, particularly regions in Arizona—the "arid zone." The heat was stifling and the resources slim, yet they managed to live in perfect harmony with it. Their stealth and warrior-ship were unparalleled, as were their stalking and hunting abilities.

Just a side note: I have first-hand knowledge of that geographic location, having lived there the first sixteen years of my life. I remember days in the summer when the temperatures soared to 110–115 degrees or higher. The nights could get very cold, dropping to the extreme. Yet, as a boy I walked for miles with bare feet and trekked and climbed mountains around the surrounding area. This could be one reason I identify with them. When you are raised in a certain location you adapt quickly as a child.

Again, most Apaches could do unbelievable things, such as run for miles in extreme heat, sometimes 50 to 80 miles. They could blend so well with the land that they could hide in broad daylight in a sparsely covered desert and not be seen. They could find water and food and often stored it for later. There is a story that goes as follows:

One day a general in the U.S. army asked one of his Indian (Apache) scouts why they couldn't find the band of renegade Apaches they were tracking.

The scout answered, "Because we can hide (disappear) and not be found, and I can prove it to you."

"How so?" the general replied.

"If you turn your back for a few seconds I will hide and you will not find me."

The general complied, for he was curious. When he turned back around the scout was nowhere to be seen. The land was barren except for a tiny scrub brush. He searched the brush and the entire area and was astonished that he was unable to find the scout. In frustration he called out for the scout. Only a few feet away, the scout arose from under the sand where he had left no marks when he hid away.

This is one reason that the Apache was such an excellent guerrilla fighter. He could spring up out of nowhere and attack ruthlessly. Most Apaches were crack shots with the repeating rifle, or any gun for that matter. They also had an uncanny spiritual connection with what they called the spirits of the land. In the mountains Geronimo hid for many months with a small band, while 5,000 soldiers combed the area. They never found him. They say he had spiritual powers, and in fact was never harmed by bullets fired at him or in any skirmishes, which were many. He finally surrendered because of the mistreatment of his friends and family.

The Apache scout was the best tracker in the world; just ask Tom Brown Jr.. Tom Brown, the world's foremost tracker and survivalist, was trained as a boy by an Apache Indian named Stalking Wolf, who was in his eighties at the time. Tom was taught to survive in the wilderness with nothing. He could be dropped off in a barren wilderness with no clothes and later come back fully clothed, armed, and well-fed. He made all of his clothes, knives, bow and arrows out of his surroundings. This is proof of the knowledge that the Apache, Stalking Wolf, passed on to him.

The Apache clothing was minimal and consisted of nothing more than knee-high moccasins, a breach cloth, shirt, and bandanna to hold back their long hair. They also wore colorful coats, shirts, beads, and jewelry. They didn't have a lot of time for religious practices because most of their time was taken up by survival. Their connection to the spirits was strong, though. Their deity was called Usen, and they usually called on the spirits of the land when needing help.

The Apache women were tough also, and were some of the best warriors. One well-known woman had the ability to feel on the skin of her arms how many of the enemy were in the area and what their location was. She was also credited with crawling into a Comanche chief's encampment and ripping out his throat with her teeth. She then stole all of his clothes and weapons and brought them back as an offering to her tribe.

22

Obviously the Apache was feared and respected by the U.S. government. But their fear overcame their respect, and since the Apache was one of the last hold-out tribes, every effort was made to either exterminate or imprison them. Geronimo himself and all the scouts who worked for the army were shipped off to Florida and imprisoned there. Geronimo never saw his beloved desert home again and died in his eighties under heavy guard on an Oklahoma reservation.

Entertainment vs. Inner Attainment

▼

SOMETIMES I WONDER IF all the lengths we go to for entertaining ourselves are really worth the trouble. We live in a world of distraction, some of it purposeful. We baby-sit our minds with some type of chattering device like TV and radio, or we have our favorite type of music playing in the background. Then we play with our toys of technology. Is this the Zen of distraction?

A lot of people are in a set routine or rut with their lives. This is not entirely their fault, but a product of social conditioning. My father had a saying: "A rut is nothing but a grave with both ends knocked out." You might get up, turn on the TV and listen to the latest bad news while brushing your teeth or preparing breakfast. Traffic reports, accidents, bad weather, and the same old crap, different day. But let's keep that mind busy with chatter so we don't hear that small, still voice of reason.

Let's just keep on that treadmill of distraction so we have no time to go to that spirit within. Some people are afraid of their thoughts, so they are stuck in that mode of keeping the "bad" thoughts subdued by entertainment. What they don't realize is that the stuff they listen to is probably putting more bad thoughts in their mind.

Particularly the bad news, TV, and commercials that support our so-called entertainment.

So how do we switch from entertainment to inner attainment, the latter being the by-passing of fearful or confusing thoughts, and getting to the bedrock of spirituality, which is silence. One small step at a time, that's how. Because if you were to suddenly disconnect from everything that surrounds you, it could be a shocking experience. It would be like plunging into a pool of very cold water. My suggestion is this. Try doing without one form of distraction for an hour, a day, or whatever is comfortable for you. Replace it with some form of stillness or meditation, or moving meditation.

Another suggestion would be to slowly change forms of entertainment to something more calm, like reading a good book, one that will perpetuate your goals of inner attainment. Or how about the reconnection to nature and all the natural forms of entertainment which are really a stepping stone to inner attainment? We have myriads of thoughts, images, and other garbage poured into our minds every day. Why don't we slowly replace or dump out that stuff? Get into creative projects that really make you feel good (god) and give you a sense of peace. Don't just listen to music, play it.

Getting back to the analogy of that pool of cold water, dip your toe or foot in first and slowly wade in until the pool is no longer a shock, but a refreshing change for the better. Disconnect from the illusion of fun and connect with the essence of bliss. Don't condemn yourself for your habits, because they do serve somewhat of a purpose. The way this world is structured, we need to have something to keep us from the insanity of everyday life. It's a way to cope and survive. But what is survival if you don't have inner serenity and peace? As wise King Solomon said, "It's all a striving after the wind." Make the changes by doing everything in moderation. Even changing to good practices and habits has to be done in moderation.

It's something to think about, food for thought if you will. Come up with your own ideas and plans on how to do it. Try it, you'll like it.

Sitting Bull and His Butterfly Hat

▼

SITTING BULL WAS A great spiritual visionary; he saw and drew pictures of the Battle of Little Big Horn before the events took place. He was a careful man regarding his people, whom he loved. Some wonder what the significance of the monarch butterfly was on his hat. The butterfly represents transformation and joy, as well as dancing. It is thought that Sitting Bull's butterfly was part of his "Medicine" and his spirit guide. I know one thing, all of Great Spirit's creatures meant and still mean a lot to the Native American way of life. I have always been inspired by the life of Sitting Bull; may he live forever in our hearts.

Spirits of the Four Directions

▼

To ATTEMPT TO WRITE on this subject is to walk a fine line, and a major undertaking! Why? Because of the personal significance it may have to any one individual, tribe, nation, etc. That being said, I am guided to proceed anyway. First, there is power in the number four. Four shows up everywhere in Native American culture. It also seems to be a universal number, appearing in other teachings and rituals, like those in the Jewish tradition, particularly the Cabala's teaching of the four angels. Then in the Bible we have Yeshua (Jesus) picking his apostles, starting with four and increasing by four until he has twelve; twelve being equally divisible by four. Part of the ritual associated with The Elders, or Pipe Carriers in the Lakota, and other traditions is to call upon the Spirits of the Four Directions.

These are as follows: Sapa, Luta, Gi, and Okaga Ska. This would be West, North, East, and South, respectively. The colors being black, red, yellow, and white. Each direction has its own meaning and power. West (Sapa) is a place where the Thunderbeings (Wakinyan) reside and is considered a place of darkness. This darkness is in a good sense, like that of solitude or meditation and crossing into the spiritual realm. North (Luta) is a place of renewal and is represented by the color red. East (Gi) is a place of brightness, light, clarity, and fire, with the color being yellow. And South (Okaga Ska) is a place or door between the spirit world and the visible realm, represented by the color white. This circle represents the cycle of life from birth, youth, to elder and death.

Some tribes vary the colors, animal representations, and meaning, but one thing for sure; the spirits of the four directions are powerful and are waiting to be called upon for direction and help. Walking the wheel of the four directions in this life can mean you have experienced many cycles of birth and death to former aspects of yourself. This is a natural thing from which we learn lessons and gain wisdom. When we gain enough wisdom we can help others walk the circle and follow ritual. We become elders in a figurative and real sense. Some are called and hear the calling. We carry the pipe, hawk or eagle feather, and drum so we may connect and heal with their use. We use sage a lot, along with various other herbs.

Some liken the spirits to the archangels of Michael, Gabriel, Uriel, and Raphael. My own personal take is that these angels have the same properties of the four directions in Native American culture. Uriel is known as the fire of God, and seems to correlate with the Thunderbeings. Raphael is a healer and could be the same as Gi or the spirit of the north who rejuvenates or renews. Gabriel could be the keeper of the spirit world or Okaga Ska (South) and Michael can be seen as the rising sun (east) or Son (Clarity) of god. This is my personal vision.

These beings or angels are all beyond gender but all are spiritual warriors and guides. How often do you call on them to help you walk the Red Road? They all have gifts for you depending on what circumstance you find yourself in. Call on them and they will be by your side instantly. Yes, you can even feel them! But you have to respect and honor them by being open-minded to their presence.

They may send someone to you on the earthly plane, kind of like an undercover angel! Is it real? That's for you to decide. Have you ever had someone appear in your life and say something helpful, and then be gone, never to be seen again? All these forces are in unison with Grandfather Sky and Grandmother Earth, which represent the masculine and feminine aspects of the universal mind or spirit.

When loading the sacred pipe, part of the ritual is to say "There is a place in this pipe for you" to each of the directions and Grandmother and Grandfather. The smoke that rises carries your prayer to Grandfather and all associated with him on a spiritual and earthly level. Don't be surprised to see a hawk or other majestic winged one fly overhead to carry the word. Build yourself a medicine wheel with a colored rock in each of the assigned four directions. Buy the books *The Sacred Pipe* by Black Elk or *Seeker of Visions* by Lame Deer. Become an apprentice to the tried and true ways of old. Also, I might mention that the colors black, yellow, red, and white represent the colors or races of mankind working as one, or being one. All my relations! The original inhabitants were called "Human Beings," or people of the earth, because they lived in harmony with it. There are no wannabees, there are only those who are and those who are not walking the Red Road regardless of race. If you like, you can call it the good road, or earth road, but I call it red because red represents renewal and rebirth.

But all man, or two-legged ones, along with the four-legged ones, winged ones, and plant life, are all related. We are all one. All my relations! My writings and words are for many purposes—some apparent and some not so apparent—but spirit asks and I write. It is good. Hecheto welo.

Giving and Receiving

▼

I HAVE RECENTLY HAD THE PRIVILEGE of experiencing generosity, support, and donations from various people who have received benefit from my thoughts and council. I want to thank them! Some have been through incredible adversity. For the record, adversity sometimes brings out the best in people. The times are trying, and situations difficult. I am very happy people have been contacting me for an exchange of healing energy. Their donations and support allow me to help them and others, but I always will and have helped, regardless.

The nation and world finds itself in circumstances that are putting a lot of pressure on the "family" of man in general. And that is exactly what we all are, "family!" Those who are perceptive on a spiritual level realize that the current monetary situation, which has and will affect us all, is an awakening of sorts. This awakening comes through the realization that the pursuit of money (the green frog skin) is not what this existence is all about. Greed and living the so-called "high life" at the expense of others has opened a Pandora's box and is bringing realization and enlightenment regarding what is really important in life. Just because the people in power have created chaos by their greed, doesn't mean that we as "The Family" (all of my relations) have to follow suit.

This is the very time when we should realize that the tradition of the "give-away" in Native American tradition is exactly what is going to heal and help all concerned. Giving comes in many forms. Giving of love, compassion, and understanding, as well as sharing on a monetary level. We need to all "hold hands" and walk the Red Road together.

It's amazing to me that the media and others keep bombarding us with bad news and negativity on the one hand, while on the other they are still trying to tell us to go out and pursue the temporary fix of material mind excitation. The talking heads tell us how bad and dire things are, and the commercials tell us to go out and take a trip to the Caribbean or buy the latest SUV or other pricey possessions.

The whole system is based on the rich riding on the backs of the poor. Go out and work hard, pay your taxes, and stay on the treadmill, and then lose everything, including your retirement, house, and nest egg, in a blink of an eye. This was never intended for us by Great Spirit. The intention was for us to live in accordance with Grandmother Earth and to receive her bounty. Each man should have his own connection with the earth, or "live under his own vine and fig tree."

So what do we do now? We band together and form circles of friends who re-establish the practice of the natural order of life. We should give from the heart and we will receive from Great Spirit through others. Give possessions, love, or just good thoughts to others. It feels damn good and is a healing in itself. It's no wonder things are the way they are when some relinquish their personal power, spirit, and soul, to those who have no soul. I have enormous empathy for my brothers and sisters who are suffering. It doesn't help to be stuck in the anger mode at those who may have caused this mess, or ourselves for buying into it. Love is required and necessary all the way around. Look at this as an event that could be the best thing that ever happened.

Start today and experience the incredible good feelings linked to giving, loving, and feeling compassion for others. There is nothing in this world that we can take with us into the next except our spiritual evolution. I will continue to give to others through my writing energy and whatever else I can come up with. I just want you all to know that I am thankful for your trust and positive energy in whatever form it takes. The fact that you read and consider my thoughts helps me fulfill what I consider to be my purpose in life.

The Drum Circle

I WENT TO THE PARK TODAY with the intention of seeing if the sick
rabbit I found the other day was OK! I had done a little feather ritual
on it the day before. He was gone, so he is either OK or crawled
away somewhere! Hopefully he is healed. As I was sitting in my
sacred space in the thick foliage, something directed my steps up the
hill. I heard drums in the distance. Was I having a vision? I started
to walk towards the sounds, and as I got closer I saw that it was a
drum circle with at least 10 to 15 drummers. All kinds of people
with various drums. I had my staff and walked closer in. I started
chanting and pounding my staff on the ground. I got good vibes so
I chanted, "Mitakuye Oyasin. Hi ye yoh hey yoh hey hey!" The vibe
picked up. There was a drum sitting on the edge of the circle. I gravi-
tated toward it. It was huge! It was a thunder drum! It was 4 feet tall
by at least 12 to 13 inches wide. It looked African! A fellow close
by told me to play it. I fell into the cacophony of rhythms. I laid
down a tribal riff, using my left hand with clenched fist (boom) and
my right open palm, slapping in alternate strokes. The ground was
literally shaking. I increased my chanting and playing. The drummers
were all one with me, increasing the rhythm to a fever pitch. I knew
none of these people, but yet I knew them all… They were all my
relations. There were women, children, Anglos, Hippies, Hispanics,
Native Americans, old, young, and a guy in a wheelchair. There were
all kinds of drums, rattles, and shakers. The more I chanted the more

the excitement increased. People were going tribal, with women, children, and men dancing in the middle. I played for two, maybe three hours full on.

As I left, one of the lead drummers shook my hand and said "What's your name?"

"I'm Thunderhands, some call me Thunder," I said.

He had a big smile, and said to come back next Sunday. I was exhausted! Still, I floated home. As I was walking home two hawks flew overhead. When I got home I threw the I-Ching (Chinese Oracle) and it came up with two hexagrams. Number two "the creative" and number eight "holding together" or "creating union with others." Does it get better than this? I had to write this! This is a true story! Only the names have been changed to protect the innocent [laughs]. Feb 22? Twenty-two is my numerological number—22/4.

A Song of Healing

▼

I AM A SPIRITUAL BEING in a divine universe.

All events and lessons in life are for my benefit.

I have reverence and gratitude for all that is.

I am quiet, still, and calm, while retaining presence of mind.

I use all perceived adversity to gain strength.

I choose to walk the Red Road of goodness.

I ask and allow the Great Spirit that moves in all things to move through and with me, for illumination on the path.

I am one with this universal spirit of healing energy.

I accept the healing, compassion, and love received and share it with all creation in heaven and earth. To the winged ones, the two- and four-legged, Grandmother Earth and Grandfather Sky.

I am a positive participant in the circle of life.

I walk the medicine wheel with all my relations.

Mitakuye Oyasin

Transforming
Hate into Love

▼

WHEN YOU HATE ANOTHER, the hatred will consume you until you become captivated by it. In a sense you become the hated and take on their persona. Sometimes this will lead you into the realization that they are none other than yourself, because we are all one.

What you hate you must love, which brings about a transformation, and rebirth. If you continue to hate, you are hating yourself, which brings grief to your spirit. This brings about confusion and leads to self-destructive tendencies. Why hate when you can love? Love feels good (god) and is in alignment with, or feeds off of, spirit or higher self.

To love is to bring balance to your soul and a clarity and purpose to your life. It elevates you towards the higher plateau called enlightenment and sets your moccasins on the right path.

Don't make hate an enemy, but see it as an opportunity or sign to shape-shift into love. "It's all about energy." When hate is directed your way you may not feel it or notice it (unless you're highly attuned) because of the way it can be masked. So practice being in a loving space and having a loving aura or energy field. This will set up a protective barrier which will repel or transmute any negative energy into light. Then the person projecting hate will get a bounce back of love instantly. This is a way we heal our fellow man and protect ourselves, with a transformation and redirection of energy.

What Your Reality
Can Teach You

▼

LET YOUR REALITY BE bio-feedback for your spirit. How much of
your mind is physical or carnal and how much is spirit? Let objects
that surround you remind you of your different sides. Everything is a
reflection of you. All situations, objects, friends and family, the clutter
in your house, the sounds outside… everything.

What you see, hear, and feel indicate what your mind is projecting
onto the field of phenomena in this illusion or dream (Maya) we call
life. Let your higher self reflect through your mind more clearly by
removing thoughts and preconceptions. Give objects outside of yourself a power or meaning that will enable your spirit.

Does that statue you have of Quan Yin really make you feel the
compassion and mercy of the feminine side of the universal mind, or
does it just sit there like a lump of clay or pottery?

Even what people say could be you projecting thoughts on them.
Imagine what the world would look, sound, and feel like if your
mind was no mind, but pure spirit. Would you see everything as
crystalline, and with an aura of energy? Would your environment be
more natural and less man-made? When you look at the picture of

life, what comes to mind? Could you re-frame the picture so that it appeals to or feeds your spirit?

What wolf do you feed: the spirit wolf or the carnal wolf? Feed the spirit wolf more and the carnal wolf less, or just enough to keep one foot in the physical world while you are really walking in the spiritual. Your mind is like an auto-pilot programmed from birth. Take it off the programmed mode and push the clear button; and from this moment on let spirit be the program for your auto-pilot. Let the universal mind guide you to the friendly skies and fly united with the spirit that moves in all things.

Ride above yourself and watch your body and world from a higher place where the red-tailed hawks fly. Ride on the wave of the ultimate ocean of spirit and pure wisdom. Become a vessel for the creative energy to flow into. Being receptive is embracing the goddess energy. Be the little yin in the big yang (see yin yang sign), and the little yang in the big yin. Let the balance, which is inherent in your true nature, be evident in your life.

You will still have lessons to learn, but won't be overwhelmed. The lessons become easier as we become more refined and balanced. The more you temper the sword of the spirit, the sharper it becomes. This will allow you to cut through the obstacles that appear in your life like a hot knife through butter. Remember, let your surroundings have meanings that empower you and you will notice a paradigm shift.

The Heart Flower Poem

THE THUNDER ROLLS AND Lightning strikes and sometimes our life
seems dire.

But just open your hearts and let others in—it's like kindling for
a fire.

The fire brings warmth and plenty of joy, and causes the miracle
of light.

And with this miracle comes a chain reaction, causing spirit to grow
so bright.

If you let the fire consume your fears, and burn up thoughts that
don't empower.

Out of the ashes grows a thing called love, which is like a
beautiful flower.

The Plainsmen and
The Indians

▼

"PLAINSMEN" IS A GENERALIZED TERM that could and does encompass a lot of characters. These are the people who had the grit to make their way out into the great plains, deserts, and forests of early America, Canada, and parts of Mexico. Don't look for the fainthearted in this bunch. You have everyone from Daniel Boone to Wild Bill Hickok. There were drifters, gold miners, trappers, mountain men, cowboys, gunslingers, and the strong stouthearted women who accompanied or took care of them. Even General Custer, in the earlier years, put up a defense for and learned from the "savages" at times. There were the immigrants and cattle barons, the railroaders and sod busters, and just a general mass of people looking for a better life.

It was a colorful time, when people lived hard, next to the land, and fought harsh environments. But you can imagine what the thoughts of the original inhabitants of this country were. A land that was pristine was soon over-run by all of the above. Many of the tribes tried to cope in a peaceful way but soon realized that this was all but futile, as the white man in general spoke with a forked tongue. Still, the true mountain men and plainsmen looked to bridge the gap and learn from the aboriginal people of the earth about their ways. There was an inclusion of many customs, dress, and hunting techniques from the native tribes of the different regions. Scouts and trackers learned their skills from the very people they were later to hunt down. The Red Man was willing to share and live together in many instances, until their back was against the wall.

The white man and the United States government owe these people a huge debt. If they had tried to become one with the land, and learned how to integrate with it, we wouldn't have the problems we are facing today. Yet greed got the better of most, with money, gold, and land-grabbing being the order of the day. Yet the Native American spirit is strong and many of, if not most of, our states and cities are named after tribes and people that were the original inhabitants. All in all, it was a colorful time and a part of history. Looking back, my sentiments, of course, are with the "people of the earth" and those who reached out to them by trying to learn their ways. Some even lived with them and became mixed blood. Many today are waking up to the true nature of these spiritual people and what they still might have to offer. And what is really interesting is that their bloodline extends or flows in many of the people living in the Americas today.

Loving Yourself

▼

"LOVING YOURSELF" MEANS REJOICING in the fact that you are a special person with all your perceived faults or flaws. Do you accept and embrace your shadow side, or "nagi" as it is called in the Lakota language? Do you realize that you are special and that there is no one quite like you on the planet? Do you look in the mirror and say "I love and accept you"?

What reason would there be not to think that you are as much a child of the universe, God, Great Spirit, or whatever you call the Deity, as the next person? I was telling a friend that I sometimes felt bad about the way some people might view me, or that they missed the point of my thoughts and writings; I wondered if I was communicating in a way that could help others. His reply was, "I haven't seen any perfect people walking the earth lately, and what about all the people that send you those heart-warming letters?"

I agree with the Zen viewpoint that we are all potential Buddhas or Christs, but we all are colored by social conditioning and thoughts from outside sources implanted in us since childhood. This can cause fragmentation, not being in harmony with the self. Does this mean that we should reject ourselves? Maybe we don't feel as spiritual or successful as the next guy. Does that mean we are worthless? The answer is no.

Life's lessons are valuable and can teach us how to rely on the connection with our higher self. We all are miracles and life itself is a miracle. Don't sell yourself short. There is an old movie with Jimmy Stewart called *It's a Wonderful Life*. In it, Stewart's character is taken off the planet as if he never existed, and the effect on his family and the community is sad and devastating because of the loss of his presence. This just means that we may affect people in ways we never dreamed of. It means that we all have something to give. It means we have the ability to change the planet and other people's lives for the better. Yes us! Little old me and you.

It is important to remember that when we do things that we don't like, it serves as a signpost to change course. Sometimes this can't be done overnight. After all, it took us years to get to where we are. Life is a journey; change comes quicker when we don't force things and when we acquire a healthy dose of acceptance. Just like the tide slowly erodes the cliff, we need to be like water. Mind like water, letting bad thoughts flow away. Yes, be like water, slowly wearing away your perceived bad character traits or habits, forgiving yourself when you don't instantly correct course.

Forgive yourself and others when you are disappointed. Don't carry the burden by yourself; love is all around you, but sometimes you can't see it or feel it. Quiet the mind and still the thoughts and feel the power of it, knowing that you and it are one, and that you are always loved. Cast off the feelings of not being worthy, for when you were a child you knew that you were. Regain the innocence of a babe and rejoice in your own foot or hand, or the reflection of yourself in the mirror.

Throw away the rule book; it's the spirit, not the law. When you begin to love yourself you find it easier to love others, and them you. When you do something good, remember it. It's easy to forget the good things we do. We're all that little boy or girl of innocence. It's just that we've been hurt along the way. Throw the hurt away and live life for another day.

What is Love?

▼

HAVE YOU EVER THOUGHT about love and how sometimes it is hard to describe? I have many feelings that are about love. Usually the question of it comes up when there is a lack of love in your own life, or when what you expect of others, and sometimes yourself, fails to manifest itself. So as I was thinking about love, a myriad of things started flowing into my mind. Believe me, I think the Bible writers even wrestled with what love was, even though they tried to spell it out. Here are some thoughts that came up that could or could not be love, but are maybe extensions of it. Also things came up that were not love, things related to love, etc. I will write; you decide if it helps your definition. Finally, love is just a word; it's the "feeling" that counts. Admittedly, you can't cure all of the world's ills, but you can start small, within your own circle of friends and family, and work your way out.

Love is when a soldier throws his body on a live grenade to save his fellow man.

Love is seeing a homeless person not as disgusting or a bum, but as a part of yourself that needs help.

Love is a mother instinctively holding her child to her breast to provide nourishment and nurturing.

Love is sometimes erotic.

Love is hugging your fellow man or woman.

Love is seeing the look in your pet's eyes when it is hungry or needs to go out, and you take care of it immediately.

Love comes easy for animals and hard for humans.

Love is seeing the look in your fellow man's eyes when he is hungry or needs the basic comforts of life, and not turning your back.

Love is the anticipation of things needed by others and giving it to them before they have to ask, or are afraid to.

Love is a four-letter word for something hard to explain, but you know it when you feel it or give it.

Loving is reaching inside to reach outside.

Love is not making your fellow man, friend, or family member beg you for love and/or help.

Love is forgiving your fellow man, friend, or family member when they don't give you love or help when you need it.

Love is not passing by someone in need and turning your head the other way.

Love is not using catch phrases like "I love you" or "Love from so and so" without also showing it with some type of demonstrable action.

Love is seeing all mankind as one with yourself, having empathy for their condition, and making some kind of physical or spiritual effort to change it for the better.

Love is forgiving others as many times as is needed.

Love is not giving up on others.

Love is not giving up on yourself.

Love is not judging others by our own egotistical standards, turning our backs on them, or casting them out of our circle or from society.

Love is acceptance of others' lifestyles, and personal choices, without condemnation.

Love is tolerance of others' spiritual beliefs.

Love is not trying to force your beliefs on others.

Love is saying and meaning "You don't have to pay me back."

Love comes from the heart, and never ends.

Love is a state of being.

Love is compassion, mercy, and forgiveness of ourselves and others.

Love is saying "Don't worry about it, I got it!"

Love is enabling, not disabling.

Love is seeing all others as Family.

Love is making room for others when there is no more room.

Love is feeling lighter when you give and heavier when you don't.

Love is considering how our words and actions might affect others.

Love is knowing that one act of kindness toward another could change both your whole life and the life of someone else.

Love is not reading into someone's words or tone of voice something bad, but giving him or her the benefit of the doubt.

Love is something that can come through you and to others from the universal mind and return to you from others.

Love is something that requires nothing other than opening up your heart to it.

Love given from the heart feels damn good to give and receive and is healing.

Love not given from the heart, but out of guilt or a sense of obligation, is not love.

Love doesn't give out of self-righteousness.

Love lifts the spirit of the giver and receiver.

Love is a feeling and an energy.

Love is not taking credit for things, but giving credit to others, or to the source of all good things.

Love should be given at any time under any condition.

Love heals giver and receiver.

Love is what you see in your fellow man's eyes when you love him.

I think I could go on forever, or for a very long time, but in case my words didn't cover it all (and I didn't) then maybe these will. A very wise man once said, "Treat others the way you would want to be treated," and "Love your neighbor as yourself." Notice it says love yourself, which is a presumption that you should already be doing that.

The Zen Teachings
of Jesus (Yeshua)

▼

WHEN JESUS SPOKE OF THE CHILD and becoming as a child, he was very much in line with Zen thought. We lose the virtue of the child mind as we gain greater dependence on spoken language and become more aware of the world. As a result of outside controls which are introduced by words and enforced by some type of threat, we begin to trust our own instincts less, with the result being the creation of a dualistic mind. Many of us also lose that sense of self-worth.

This divides the inner from the outer, me from you, and in the larger sense, good from evil, etc. The young child's mind is like a clear glass of water that becomes polluted with external worldly rules, concepts, dogma, and societal conditioning in general. We eventually loose touch with that kingdom within.

The Zen term of "Mushin" refers to original mind, empty mind, or child's mind. We are born enlightened and spend our whole life trying to get back to that state of mind. Guilt, fear, anger, and a lot of other negative emotions come from indoctrination and a muddying of the water. It's no wonder that Christ said, "Unless you become as a child you shall not see the kingdom of God." Couple that with his words of "The Kingdom of Heaven is within you," and you have one of the most advanced Zen teachings known.

Is Jesus a Zen master or are Zen masters exemplars of Christ? It matters not, for universal law is universal law. Jesus was an enlightened being, or master; master of himself, master of the universe, and teacher of "The Way." Christians who worship or go to church but don't catch the true meaning behind his words, failing to even try to comprehend what he was teaching, are just going through the paces. Worse yet, they may be projecting belief systems that are diametrically opposed to what Yeshua stood for. I guess that's why we should heed the admonition of being "aware of false prophets" or "wolves in sheep's clothing." This not to say there are no "sincere Christians."

It is not for me to judge. However, most Christian religions and churches indoctrinate and lay guilt on people, as well as cause a lot of hate and fear. This is not conducive to having a child's mind, as spoken about by Yeshua. Why follow empty rhetoric and dogmatic teachings when you can go directly to the source and receive direct transmission?

My Prayer to Earth Mother

Earth Mother, you are the sacred feminine, the female aspect of the universe. Open your arms and embrace me. Send the healing force of nature to be my companion. Raise my spirit with your nurturing presence. Guide my feet as I walk on your fertile ground. Unite me with the Spirit that moves in all things. Show me the path of the Red Road. Balance my body, mind, and soul, and ground me in your love, mercy, and compassion. Give me the strength to move upward like a seedling making its way to the sun. Calm and clear my mind like the surface of a smooth pond. Give me a firm foundation like the majestic mountains that endure through the ages. Make my heart soft like the snowflakes that fall from the misty clouds of your breath. Protect and shelter me like a bear in its cave of hibernation. Renew me like the cherry blossoms of spring. I honor you for your wisdom and thank you for it. May I be one with all that is your creation.

Trust and Gratitude

SOMETIMES WE JUST HAVE TO trust the higher power, our higher selves, or Great Spirit, for guidance. Times can be really tough and events can trigger us into feeling down or unhappy. When we are in these situations we try everything we can to advance correctness, but sometimes we run into obstacles. To put it simply, we try too hard. When faced with this situation, retreat and take a rest. Give it up to the higher power for a while, with trust that it will work out.

If possible, keep the ego uninvolved by stilling restless thoughts. Once we identify something that needs to be corrected in ourselves or others, gentle but ceaseless penetration is the key. Like the wind blowing steadily in the same direction, wearing away doubts and inferior ego-driven qualities.

At times of darkness, gratitude for all the good things in your life can bring in some light. Just remember that you are one with the higher power who embodies the father, mother, and eternal love. You have spiritual help all around you and it doesn't hurt to ask or pray for help. Don't try to do it all yourself. Let go of any dark thoughts and aggressive attempts to make things right. Be grateful for the lessons that can redirect your path to a more beneficial outcome.

Surviving the World's Perfect Storm

A HIGH PERCENTAGE OF SOULS in the world right now are angry, scared, and apprehensive about the future. Anger, fear, and other negative emotions abound everywhere. There seems to be an overwhelming amount of pressure on the inhabitants of this wonderful planet Earth. You might even call it a worldwide "perfect storm." An analogy might be found in the movie called *The Perfect Storm*, in which a series of meteorological events caused a horrendous and destructive storm. The series of events happening in this world right now have reached this high magnitude. An aware person certainly might ponder the outcome and wonder what they can do to "ride this one out."

The elements that make up the storm can be summed up largely with three words: Decrease, Opposition, and Return. Let's take the first element of "decrease." We see significant evidence of decrease in all areas of life. The financial global markets are, to put it bluntly, crashing. This causes a decrease in all of the other areas, a domino effect if you will. One of the dominoes is a decrease in tolerance, which results in anger and fear. Another component of this perfect storm is the political climate, which by a strange twist of fate, is happening at the same time as the decrease. The world political climate can be considered a component of "opposition." This opposition is fueling the fire of anger, hatred, racism, and religious intolerance. This is done by stirring up our most basic and primal fears of anyone who might be considered different, or a threat to our survival. The third element of the storm—"return"—is cyclical change. Change is a fact of life, but this cyclical change is the ending of the old and the beginning of the new.

Now the "decrease" part of the storm can be largely attributable to the souls who inhabit this planet and live in this world. Decrease comes when there is too much increase; a re-balancing. The increase we are talking about in this instance was an increase in the egotistical elements of greed, false pride, and materialism. The "opposition" element is connected with the political, ideological, and religious (not spiritual) components of our world, and is showing itself in very ugly and angry ways. Again we have the emotion of anger being a particularly destructive component of this storm.

Let's talk about the element of "return" or cyclical change for a moment. In a normal world and planet, this is a natural thing and takes different forms. However, because of the aforementioned components of greed, false pride, and materialism, the planet may be forced into a premature or early cyclical change called global warming. The greenhouse effect, global warming, and pollution of the planet are all the results of the self-centered thought, "Grab all you can, while you can." This attitude of the powers that be, or the world's leaders, is without regard to our natural habitat. The rich get richer (materialism) and the earth suffers in return. The good people on the planet who have mistakenly put their faith, future, and protec-tion in other people's hands are having a rude awakening right now; the result being more anger and fear.

It isn't a very cheery scenario or picture, I know. But there are measures that you can take to protect your sanity, and remain centered and calm. In fact if you look at the situation from a different point of view, you have the possibility to emerge from this period of time stronger, healthier, and wiser. You may ask, how?

Again I will use the analogy of the storm: "Batten down the hatches." What does this mean in real terms? Simply this: "Go within." When they batten down the hatches on a ship they go within for protection. Your goal should be to stay in the eye of the hurricane and not the wall. The I-Ching, an ancient Chinese Oracle, has all of the aforementioned terms of Opposition, Decrease, and Return as names for hexagrams (64 in all) of cyclical change, and phases we may experience.

The I-Ching is like receiving advice from a wise master, your higher self, or the deity of your choice. In times of decrease it advises us to "Be still, lessen the power of the ego, and misfortune will be avoided." When our resources are limited and difficulty surrounds us, our egos generate angry and unhappy emotions. This also happens when we are unable to achieve our goals. In the current political climate this is evident. One side may think that their ship is going down and their egos become infuriated. This hardens them so much that they propagate and display anger and bitterness. Also, because of this intense world situation, in most people's personal lives this same scenario and reaction is taking place. In other words, they find opposition affecting them and their relationship with others. Do you see what I mean by the perfect storm?

Take the advice of the wise sage. Be still, meditate, and "return" to your quiet center, like a spring returns to the inside of a mountain during a time of drought. Withdraw from the media, newspapers, and negative influences. If you find yourself screaming at someone on TV, turn it off. Sacrifice the ego, for it is powerless against the currents of life. You can't force progress by arguing, manipulation, or making excuses. In a sense you are retreating to the calm eye of the hurricane, instead of getting caught in the wall, and are flowing with the storm until it dissipates.

The I-Ching also speaks of this opposition. I quote: "Misunderstanding truth creates opposition." You might add "distorting truth" to this also. It speaks of events in life which can tempt us into negative thoughts and mistrust of others. It can cause us to mistrust life and believe that it is working against us. The lessons that we and the planet as a whole are experiencing are lessons that we need at this time in our evolutionary journey. Whatever is happening now must happen. We can't resist, because even if we try we can't prevent the progress of cyclical changes that must take place. It's time to display our higher and more loving aspects of ourselves. Transmute the anger and hatred to love and let go of dark thoughts and aggressive actions. Embody the sage, Jesus, or some other high spiritual person or purpose that is your ideal. It's time to strengthen your inner light and reserves.

The I-Ching's comments about "return" offer a positive possibility to this story. It says, "A time of darkness comes to an end." This is a turning point, the greatest adversity can be put behind us and the light can return. It warns that it can't be forced, and so you might as well rest and act only when you can move gently and innocently. Return also means to return to the light within yourself. Growth is only possible when we relinquish the expressions of the ego: pride, impatience, anger, and desire. Let things develop naturally in their own way. "Simply observe and accept changes as you observe and accept the rising of the sun." Gather your strength for a new growth ahead and a return to the light. It's up to you as an individual and all of us collectively to change our consciousness, or it will be changed for us.

Life is a Journey

▼

Like a good friend said to me today, "It's not the negatives and the positives that define life; they might make life more interesting and bring out different aspects, but its all about the journey." We truly are wanderers or travelers on this road we call life. The bumps in the road definitely push us toward a more reflective mode. But no matter what comes our way, we have to be flexible and flow around the obstacles instead of beating our head against them. It's this allowing the flow of the river to push us along that puts us in touch with the Tao and Great Spirit. When I was a pilot and flight instructor, it was understood that the first instinct when you hit turbulence is to fight it. But the best method to get out of that situation is not to fight it or panic. It's funny how not fighting things works better than fighting. It's all about understanding resistance. Just like electricity flowing through a wire. The wire causes resistance and stops the energy from flowing as freely. But when lightning comes from the sky there is no resistance. Let your life be without resistance to the natural energy or chi surrounding us and life in general. Be like lightning. Walk what the Native American calls the "Red Road."

The Suffering of
the Masses

▼

I CAN'T LET THIS CURRENT financial situation go by without
commenting more on it. It seems history has lessons for us if we look
for them. Any empire is vulnerable when the focus of its agenda is on
the material instead of the spiritual. America has been walking a thin
line for a long time. Greed and power is the name of the game. It's a
form of gluttony. It's been that way since day one, when the peaceful
Native American inhabitants of this beautiful land were eliminated, to
a large degree, by a form of genocide. If you believe in karma, then
it's being delivered in large portions.

The general American public does not consist of graduates from an
elite school of finance and is in the dark about the intricacies of how
the system works or doesn't work. It is depending on the chiefs of
the tribe, called the government, to watch over and protect it. Now,
in contrast, you have the Indian chiefs of the Native American tribes,
who were allowed to be in their position because they proved themselves to be honorable men through years of observation by the rest
of the tribe. Where are the honorable men in our society? How do
we know who is honorable and who isn't?

A couple of quotes from different traditions are in order. "When the
evil are in power, the people suffer." (I-Ching.) "By their fruits you

shall know them." (Bible.) "Certainly they are a heartless nation, they have made some of their people servants." "The greatest object of their lives seems to be to acquire possessions—to be rich." "They desire to possess the whole world." (White Footprint-Sioux.)

The majority of American people try to do the right thing, but it seems they face oppression, panic, and fear at every turn of the road, and are, in fact, slaves. They work hard just to survive, while the leaders of the land gorge themselves on the fruits of the people's labor. This problem is deep and systemic. The American people have a gut feeling that something isn't right, and the feeling is something they should attend to; it's called intuition. There are no quick fixes to something of this nature.

It is better to take no action than the wrong action, or an action that is meaningless. I won't take sides regarding the political situation, but know this: These people (government leaders) are not stupid; they are deep into military strategy and know how to manipulate and distract the masses of people. We don't really know the inner workings of their minds other than what we can see by the results, which are evident.

I would be presumptuous to claim to have the answers, but here's a thought I've repeated often. We seem to be in a position where we have no real control other than to speak out. Try to remain calm, centered, and detached, because if there is anything that these people want, it's for you to panic so that you can be manipulated through your fear. Keep a clear head, and connect with people of like mind who know that this isn't right. We the people are collectively stronger than those who lead. It's time to band together on many levels, including the spiritual. Meanwhile the commercials wail on about all the material things we just must have now! Welcome to the reservation.

People in Panic

▼

EARLIER IN SOME OF my writings I talked about being in the world, but not of it. "The world" is in a panic about money and the economy. What does it say when people feel the need to e-mail the media and ask them what to do? What's needed is a spiritual perspective on the ebb and flow of life, including money and material things. With the majority of people in this life having some form of religious or spiritual upbringing, this question begs to be answered. Why do they depend so much on government (political figures), and the media, to supply them with consolation and/or protection? Have these entities become their God? There is no solace in taking refuge in a house that is falling apart.

Just a few key words and phrases come to mind from various spiritual traditions. Don't store up your treasures where rust and moths can consume them. Practice non-attachment to everything, including your own body, on a daily basis, or at least think about it. The Tao Te Ching speaks of change and cycles and how inevitable these things are. The time has come to ask if you are watching this from a detached position, or are getting caught up in a struggle against inevitable events? Making the government, the media, and even external religions your basis for protection and spiritual solace may not be the best approach. We all are tempted to get caught up in the vicissitudes of life, yours truly included. In a nutshell, this makes things more painful. The government, media, and religion are like the Wizard of Oz. Much ado about nothing. In other words, for all practical purposes, look behind the face they are wearing.

Has past history indicated anything other than propagation of falsehood, lies, and deceit? Is this something you can count on when the chips are down? The bottom line is to start today with a new realization, because everything you need is within you. Look inside, not outside. The kingdom of heaven is within, if you will. Meditation, prayer, and genuine reflection are my recommendation. Go to the well of spirituality and solace within, because out in the world promises made are not promises kept. My prayers and thoughts are with my fellow man, and my hopes are that this will be an awakening of some sort as to what the real priorities are in life. Don't get caught up in "Maya," or the illusion we call life.

The Feminine Aspect of the Universe and The Tao

▼

I LOVE THE GODDESS ASPECT of the universe. The Tao Te Ching says, "It (the Tao) is the unlimited father and mother of all limited things." Picture two photos of the goddess aspect being portrayed. One with the dragon (Taoist) and the other with the Thunderbird or Thunderbeings (Native American). We also have many other examples, such as Kwan Yin, who is a goddess of mercy, and the White Buffalo Woman, who gave the Native American the red stone pipe. Grandmother or Mother Earth comes to mind, also. Certainly these cultures realized the importance of the soft and yielding manner of the Yin energy. With this comes the gift of compassion and mercy. It would be beneficial for any society, especially those of a patriarchal nature, to recognize and embrace the dual aspect of nature and the universe. This should also be recognized within oneself. Another quote from The Tao Te Ching of Lao Tzu: "To know the masculine and yet cleave to the feminine is to be the womb of the world." Indeed, we could use a more soft, yielding atmosphere in the world we see around us.

Gods, Goddesses, and Deities

▼

JUST WHAT ARE THESE gods and/or archetypes, and where do they come from? If you asked Joseph Campbell (one of the world's foremost authorities on mythology), he would say that gods, goddesses, and deities are something that men, women, tribes and cultures in different periods of time created or manifested through their connection to the collective unconscious.

So, in my way of thinking, the Greeks have Zeus, the Jews Yahweh, the Chinese a pantheon of gods and goddesses. They again were thought of and/or infused into an existing real person. Things become legend and take on a life of their own. So, to make a long story short, we (humankind) created gods or aspects of the one universal force—or the Tao—because It (The Tao) can't be named. These creations, or gods, are us, really, or aspects of ourselves or higher selves.

How real can they become? Maybe as real as we want or need them to be. For instance, if a deity or god or immortal, such as Kwan Kun, was created for protection, then maybe that thought, perpetuated over thousands of years, has quite a bit of power. Of course anything has as much power as you want to give it. So with those thoughts in mind, maybe we should use these external projections to our advantage, like we do with the immortals of feng shui. In a sense it is a universal mind game on a high level. What's fascinating to me is the fact that many of these gods or goddesses appear in similar forms within cultures or peoples that never knew each other. So it has to come from the collective unconscious. Now the question arises: What is this collective unconscious? Even Joseph Campbell didn't claim to really know. Is it the great mystery? The Tao? The Great Spirit that moves in all things? Yes, that's my best guess. I would like to think that it is projecting these myths and archetypes on us for our benefit. Feng shui is common sense, geomancy, a science. But it is a belief system too. It's good to believe in a protecting deity or guardian. The mind is powerful and can use the imagery of that god for our benefit.

Healing and Addictive Thinking

▼

THE EGO MAY FEEL THREATENED if it were to not have some of its addictive and compulsive thinking. On the other hand, your true self may feel a whole lot better if you didn't have this way of thinking coloring the world. It would be like lifting a burden from your shoulders and removing something that might be blocking an energy channel in your aura. This could then even be manifesting as that sensation in your physical being. Letting go of this thread of preconditioning could free you of tension in your body.

Is this going to be a difficult thing, ridding yourself of this thinking addiction? Maybe it boils down to: just how difficult do you want it to be? Sometimes you might have to form an alliance with your ego and higher self. Make an agreement that you will be gentle with the ego. Don't start a war within yourself. Make a bridge between the ego and your higher self, or "sage" self. All relationships take time to develop. Should the one within be any different? Work with it at your own speed. As you continue this "awareness in the moment" process, over time things become easier. You begin to see more clearly the patterns of addictive thought. You begin to see a cause and effect. Not just with thinking, but with your physical addictions as well.

Just remember as you practice this awareness process not to judge, condemn, or beat yourself up. Chances are that whatever it is that is manifesting in your life that's not serving your best interests might have come from a lack of compassion or love in the first place. So give yourself plenty of love. This is a good way to heal and become enlightened in the process. To me, being enlightened is removing the heavy load and becoming a lighter being, or light being. So ponder these thoughts, and begin a new journey as a wanderer and "wonderer" of life. Make this the first day of a new healing journey and a new life. The life you really want.

In the World but Not of It

▼

THIS THOUGHT IS KIND OF an extension of previous thought and
could be an ongoing topic, but I don't think that far ahead. Reading
my previous writings might give you a little more insight into
this one.

So we are continuing on the premise that we are a product of social
conditioning since birth, from all the input of the "world" around us.
And that this is what created our ego and all our supposed wants and
needs. Let's look at our thinking, and the possibilities surrounding
that process. As we live in the awareness of the moment we notice
thoughts arising about our experience. And as we look or reflect on
these thoughts, while viewing the flow of them with no judgment,
we start getting closer to our "essence" by realization.

We should have a "wondering attitude" about what is creating our
feelings, sensations, and thoughts about the present moment. Pictures
or images may arise from what's coming up. Again, let these images
come gently, like bubbles rising to the surface of a pond. You might
have a sudden awakening. You could see things that astound you.
You might even say things like, "Wow! Now I see why I feel this
way about what I am experiencing." You might see an incident in
your life that is triggering the emotional response you're having at
the moment. Sensations could arise in your body. Whether they are

pleasurable or not, let thoughts about them float to the surface. Are you causing this pleasure or pain because of an earlier event?

Suppose you say yes, an event happened when I was 12 years old. The question then arises: But how could that event have anything to do with my preconditioning? I was past my formative years. OK, so take that event and trace it back further. Don't force it; just let it happen. As you trace this "thread" back (and this could happen all in just a few moments or minutes) you begin to see that there might be a pattern of addictive thinking, or a series of events. The real kicker comes when you have a vision of what might have been the original stimuli that caused this thread of events, and/or addictive thinking. You might also see how this pattern is something that became part of the ego. It might be such an entrenched part of your ego that it (your ego) makes you feel like you need it. I have been thinking about the phrase "in the world but not of it." Where did this thought come from and what does it mean to you and me? First let me start by saying that the thought has been around for a long, long time and is found in many ancient wisdom traditions, including Sufism, Christianity, and others. There is a Biblical reference to it in Jesus' words in Romans. To me this may be a key to life, if not *the* key. Right away, the I-Ching hexagrams "The Traveler or Wanderer" and "The Caldron" come to mind.

How do we journey through this life, living and functioning in this world, but not be of it? I think the meaning of it goes a lot deeper than people might realize. I don't pretend to know what the exact answers are, but maybe I can give some insight from my perspective. I mentioned the hexagram (56) of the I-Ching called "The Traveler or Wanderer" and (50) "The Caldron." However, the whole I-Ching, and a lot of other holy books, might be trying to point us to the way of achieving or returning to this state of not being "of the world."

What is your world from a subjective point of view? I would put forth the notion that the world as we see it is a reflection of everything that is inside us, as well as that of the collective consciousness surrounding us. When we are children or newborns we are closer to, or are, the pure essence, like a sparkling glass of clear water. As we become socially conditioned, our pure essence becomes integrated with thoughts and projections from other entities. These range from our parents to schools and religious institutions. As we progress through life, everything is colored by these; let's call them introduced impurities. To put it simply, we forget who we are and become involved with the drama of life.

Our original essence and our connection to the ultimate essence is corrupted and made impure. We form what is called an ego, or false perception of who we are and what might really be important. Once this ego is formed it seeks to propagate itself with things that please it or make it feel comfortable. But do we really feel comfortable? Aren't we always searching to improve, keep our lot in life, or the status quo? As we approach the later years of life, questions can really start cropping up. For instance, "What's this all for? Where am I headed?" When the "world gets chaotic, and the people around us seem like strangers" we start asking the hard questions.

It's at this time that we realize that our involvement with "the world" may be an illusion. And that, my brothers and sisters, is exactly what it is. For the essence of your true self is a light that has been

covered a long time ago. How do we "return" to our true pure selves
and uncover the light? Maybe this could be called re-enlightenment
instead of enlightenment.

The I-Ching says we are wanderers or travelers, as in a foreign
country. This hexagram, called "Lu" in Chinese, reminds us that
we should be traveling through life like we are traveling through
a foreign country. Strangers in a foreign land are careful not to get
sidetracked into difficult situations or fall in with unsavory characters.
The I-Ching hexagram "The Caldron" talks about sacrificing our ego
and accepting guidance from a higher power.

Let's put this into a real-time scenario. When we perceive anything
in this so-called world, do we become emotionally involved and let
our senses, instead of our "essence," rule us? Maybe the key is living
life from a detached or non-attached point of view. Everything we
see before our eyes and feel with our senses is, in fact, programmed
illusions or perceptions. These are based on that belief system being
formed since childhood.

So we walk down the street and see, for instance, a homeless person.
We might have several feelings come up, such as feelings of hurt or
feelings of fear. This would depend on our personal preconditioning.
But what if we began to go through life as wise travelers, looking at
things as if they are a motion picture? A projector projecting images
on a screen. Are you doing the projecting, or maybe writing a script
to cause a phenomenon, which is really just energy and a play of
vibratory light? Because that's all "matter" or what that homeless
person really is. "The observer affects the observed." Not that you
shouldn't have compassion, or be a non-feeling person. But turn

down the volume and live life "viewing" the world, and realize it for what it is every second you're living it. The more you have awareness of the moment, and not just living in the moment, the quicker you will begin to perceive or rediscover your own essence.

It's like a smelting process. We slowly remove the impurities of our preconditioning by looking at each moment with a peaceful feeling of wonderment, and seeing the power of our own thoughts and what we can or cannot do with them. Maybe another way to put it would be to examine what kind of sensory feelings we are projecting onto ourselves, and maybe onto others, in each moment of whatever comes up in life. Be a simultaneous watcher of the world and your ego self, which essentially have become one in the same through preconditioning. Remember that our essence is pure; some might call it our spirit. And our essence doesn't have anything to do with the world, which includes even our own body. Change the way you look at (view) things and the things you look at will change. Maybe you will discover your essence in the process.

Refuge in a
Troubled World

▼

SOMETIMES INFERIOR INFLUENCES PREVAIL in this surrounding
phenomenon we call a world. Like what is described in the I-Ching,
hexagram number 12—"Pi"—which is standstill. There are other
hexagrams that are similar. Sometimes it's better to retreat into your
higher self or to be still and meditate. We try to make things right
when the flow isn't allowing us to. Why forge through the rapids
when sometimes it is better to guide your canoe over to the shore
and take a rest? Let the storm blow over and the clouds clear. This
gives us time to get out of the stream of chaotic energy surrounding
us. It gives us time to center. It also gives us time to have an empty
mind and relax. Get into the space of "not trying" by being what
I call stress-free, thought-free, mind-free, and body-free, letting go,
going on retreat. This doesn't mean you quit growing. In fact, this
gives you time to grow while everything around you is standing still,
or worse yet, in chaos. Treat yourself nicely; you deserve it. Don't let
the imbalance in the world or around you take a toll. Let Great Spirit
handle it. Sometimes we can be an inhabitant of the planet, but not
of the world, if you get my meaning!

Natural Disasters, Acts of God?

▼

It's ironic that when there is a natural disaster, people say "Oh! That was an act of God." How so, I say? Do you mean that God sits up in the sky and commands nature to wreak havoc? What's so funny is that in the context of nature, being one with the "Tao," "Great Spirit," or whatever is a comfortable name for you, it might well be called an act of God in a natural sense. Not with thought-out vengeance or purposeful harm, but as an act of the planet being herself.

Of course Mother Earth, when confronted with pollution, wars, and general destruction of her resources, would react like any living organism and proceed to correct things. How this is done might be revealing in itself. Of course there have always been natural occurrences. But when people get in the way it becomes a disaster. Some things to consider are overpopulation and what that population actually does to remain in harmony with the natural order of things. Balance inside may equal balance outside.

Native American Definition of Medicine

ALTHOUGH NATIVE AMERICANS ACCEPT the western view of the word "medicine," their understanding is much broader and encompasses a context on which their tradition is based. This can include the presence and power embodied in or demonstrated by a person, a place, an event, an object, or natural phenomenon. It can mean the power, potency, energy, or spirit of whatever event or object is being experienced—a common phrase being "that's good medicine." Seeing a hawk fly overhead while doing a ritual or prayer can be good medicine. Other things might fall into the "bad medicine" category. It really depends on the spirit involved. A medicine object can be beneficial to a healing process—things such as a feather, a crystal, etc. The term medicine man or woman can be confusing or ambiguous. There are many kinds of healers. Some use herbs, while others may use words or spiritual powers. I prefer the Lakota term "Wichasa Wakan," meaning holy or sacred man. This indicates someone who is a spiritual or a holy person who pursues and serves the sacred and divine. The divine being Great Spirit and all that is associated with the Creator of all. Birds, flowers, herbs, and nature in general embody the Spirit of the Creator. The term "medicine man" would more properly fit a grade-B western movie. The healers in the Native American community are much more diverse and accomplished than

some would believe. The western world of so-called modern medicine is starting to come to terms with other healing modalities based
in different cultures, but not fast enough.

The Integral Way

▼

THE DEFINITION OF INTEGRAL is "consisting or composed of parts that together constitute a whole." When we start cultivating ourselves we integrate with the whole and go beyond the duality. We look at the bigger picture and feel the oneness of all. This can be a healing process as we begin to go to the core level of our own being, integrating and accepting even our own feelings and parts of ourselves. This is done with no judgment and brings about a feeling of wholeness within. It also helps in the process of cultivation, as things that we do battle with no longer have a hold. They dissolve in the oneness of the whole and the negativity surrounding them disperses. When there is no opponent, there is no battle. First we integrate, then we cultivate, which brings about a natural order and balance. Cultivation is acceptance, humility, and following our superior or higher self. It's all a process. Feel the oneness of self with nature and the Tao.

Every Day is a Lifetime

▼

WHEN WE GET UP in the morning we don't know how our day will progress. That is why it is good to have an adaptable attitude. How our day progresses may have to do with how we live it; that's why we should nurture the moment. It is said that when we proceed to the next life we have no remembrance of the former. This is so we don't have too much on our mind or become overwhelmed in the life we are living. That's how we should live each day, putting away past memories and concentrating on the moment. Inferior thoughts may arise sometimes and we should retreat from them until a time when it is more beneficial to move forward. A lot of times these thoughts arise when we are accomplishing something superior or making progress along particular lines. Be aware of the moment; know when to proceed or retreat. Progress on matters important to you may seem slow sometimes. Make time work for you when working on cultivating good habits. Sometimes it's best to just bite off a little; other times you can take larger pieces. Regulation, moderation, cultivation are all good things. The less we become aroused by inferior thoughts the more balanced we will be, and life will be on more of an even footing for us. This brings a form of contentment and peace, no matter what is appearing in our lives. Look at the duality. Be like water and fill up the deep spaces slowly so you can overcome them with time, and then flow on.

Pick Your Thoughts

▼

WHAT THOUGHTS DO YOU WISH to be in your head or do you give power to? How about the thoughts you read? I have been reflecting a lot lately about what I write, and also about what I read. If you see or hear a thought that doesn't empower you or make you feel good, just look at it and let it go. With those that do make you feel better, say to yourself, "Yes, I can be empowered with that," or "That fits into my scheme of things." Thoughts are images, so maybe you want to work with a particular image in your head. Never struggle with it; just let it happen or let it go.

In my case I take myself way too seriously sometimes, as we all do from time to time. After all, Great Spirit knows I'm not a saint; and if I were, it is said that in order to be a saint you have to have been a sinner. One of my friends has a blog and at the top he has: sacred, profane, sacred, profane. I like the drift—two sides of a coin if you will. A little humor and sarcasm doesn't hurt either. So on that note I have decided to diversify a bit and start including more witty, humorous, and cynical things in my life. This will include works by Mark Twain and many others. Life's too short. Yes, I will be beating the spiritual, ecological, and ethnic drum as always, but hey—it's all good. Not that anyone takes me that seriously anyway. And if at times you encounter a little profanity in life, remember, it's one of two sides of the same coin. One thing you can be sure of, life and my writings will always be thought-provoking.

"Ta Tay" the Wind

▼

TA'TE (Ta TAY) the Wind is the Messenger of Skan, Lakota God of the sky, or the supreme authority. Sometimes Ta'te is sent to stir things up and plant new seeds. Ta'te can also be associated with storms and thunder, which have been discussed earlier in my writings. Ta'te is something that you can't see, but the effects are felt. Try standing on a bluff and let the wind clean your aura by feeling it blowing through your body and carrying away all the stress and negativity. Ta'te is what is blown through the flute and is expressed or manifested in a musical form to soothe the soul. The next time you feel the wind gently blowing across your face, think of Great Spirit.

Of course the wind can be powerful, as in a thunderstorm or tornado. That's why it's so important to live in tune with nature and (Maka) Mother Earth.

What Do You Mean Spiritual?

▼

HOW CAN YOU SEARCH for something you already are? If you're searching you're not realizing that there is no way you can "not be spiritual." Yes, You!! That's right, with all your thoughts and habits both sacred and profane, naughty and nice, good and evil, and on and on. Those are just words. Don't accept a belief and then beat yourself up and punish yourself because you didn't live up to it. Don't reject and hate others because they are different or not on your spiritual path. Get over it! Accept yourself for who you are. You started out as a beautiful child, an empty clear glass; then all this "stuff" got poured into you, stirred around and the glass became murky. After that it all settled to the bottom, and every once in a while a piece floats to the surface and you go "ouch," or you say, "That's not me!" It's all you, my friend, and there is no use in feeling guilty about all that stuff, because deep down inside *you are spiritual!* Love all parts of yourself and integrate it all, so that it empowers you.

If you happen to find a part of yourself that feels guilt, fear, and shame, let your higher self, sage self, shaman self, or whatever self you chose, intervene. Have a reasonable conversation with this doubting part. Who knows you better than you? A shrink, a guru, a minister? Not hardly! Go within and have a good lively conversation and you will realize that you are the creator. Don't feel guilty about being a spiritual being in the world's clothes. Feel good and accept and love all parts of yourself. The Lakota have a word for the ghost self (called "nagi") that wanders in limbo until you accept it, nurture it, and give it a home. The sooner you accept it, the happier you will be. You have nothing to live up to except what others have planted in your head. So yes, they planted it there and it's part of you. And yes, it's the little boy or girl feeling bad because he or she didn't live up to or try hard enough to live up to whatever it is. But the more you look at that "stuff" and the different aspects of your personality, you see more of the clear water and less of the murky stuff. Nothing is other than what you believe it to be, so just be yourself and love every bit of it. Feel good about who you are! Because in the final wash you are that clear water in the glass!

Pole Shift

▼

WHAT'S GOING ON WITH the planet, world, energy we are accustomed to? Why all the weird weather, earthquakes, tornadoes, and just the overall feeling of unease on the planet? My friends feel it. Do you? Have our imaginations gone wild? You decide. My theory is that with the latest discoveries of cracks in the polar ice cap and the melting and breaking away of some large chunks of ice, something is changing on a deeper level than some would like to admit. There is drought in a lot of areas too. This wasn't supposed to happen for decades by some accounts. Edgar Cayce and the Hopis mentioned this very thing happening around this time. The year 2012 has been mentioned and I have been asked about it. Maybe the shifting of the poles would create a time warp too! I would think anything is possible, but I will leave that to the scientists. Maybe I shouldn't, though, because their predictions and models about the ice cap and other things are way off. And I'm just talking about the natural things. We are all connected to nature so it would affect all that is around us, including our moods, and maybe our energy. Is it scary? No, but it could wreak havoc on a larger scale than what we already see. I guess we will all just have to be observers. Trying to correct this situation has been and would be a challenge. Maybe the best thing to do now is just remain optimistic because it might be for the best. I hope so for the sake of my grandchildren. Maybe it will usher in a change of consciousness and well-being. Heck, we might all get kicked into another dimension. Or maybe the original people that brought us here from the Pleiades will come down and pick us up.

Natural Resources and Man-Made Disasters

▼

Natural Resources

First I would like to touch on the natural resources portion of this article. I heard that oil could go up so high that people who drive could end up paying five to eight dollars a gallon at the pump. This will affect other modes of transportation such as trucks and trains. People are suffering, folks, and guess what? All this shortage of the natural resources, specifically oil, if in fact there is a shortage, is going to have an effect on every man, woman, and child in this country.

Higher prices will prevail in all areas that are on the tail-end of this irresponsible occurrence. High food prices occur because the trucks and trains that deliver our food won't be able to deliver. The cost of refrigeration is going up. The cost of anything made of petroleum products is going up. That would include all plastics, plastic containers, etc., in which most of our food is packaged.

This is not a time for the fainthearted. It's a time for people to wake up. Now I know I have been talking a lot about peaceful revolutions, and Gandhi-type protests and sending love. And all these things are still good, but now I am going to change the dynamic a little and partake in the duality. This is just unconscionable and totally uncalled for.

This is about survival of the poor, the elderly, those on fixed incomes, and the general population. When you look at the cost of man's inhumanity to man by the different means that have arisen, people need to do more than just speak out. They need to take matters into their own hands. War and mismanagement, along with greed, seem to be the cause of the critical situation facing us all. The effect from the phony war on terrorism in Iraq and the residual aftermath might just create chaos in America and in the world at large. I suggest families contact one another and get ready or prepare themselves for the worst. Am I buying into fear tactics being propagated by the powers that be? To quote an ancient oracle: "When the wicked are in control the people will suffer."

Man-Made Disasters

The situation in the world puts a lot of things in perspective. Now they are saying that there are millions of people homeless, and a multitude starving, with greedy governments in control that keep aid from getting where it needs to be and helping those poor souls. Think about that a minute: millions of people homeless and starving. How many more will die? If there ever were a need for readjustment, it would be to go in and clean house on the people holding up the progress of aid, welfare, and humanitarian efforts to those in need. Yes, this is a man-made disaster, but it's how you rectify these things that counts. Then there are the other changes around the world, which are already numbering a record high for this time of year.

Would you say that the planet seems a little unbalanced right now? Is it a reflection of the unbalanced consciousness of the people on Mother Earth? I will leave that for the reader to decide. I hope there is someone out there reading this and passing it on because that might be the only way my thoughts get to the public. It is up to each person on this planet to spread the word so we can form a consensus and consider possible solutions. I have been getting a lot of feedback on my writing, and I will continue to write because I care.

God, Religion, and Enlightenment

▼

OK FOLKS, THIS COULD be a long one but I will try to distill it. There has been a shift going on in what I have perceived lately regarding Jesus, whose real name is Yeshua, or Yehoshua. Or maybe it is a shift in the whole spiritual view of religions, particularly Christianity, and God. My take on it has been one that has grown over the years, but as of late it has acquired new dimensions through self-realization, meditation, and a whole lot of reading. Instead of making statements, I will ask questions and make statements you can ponder. Let's start with Yeshua. He was a rebel, an apostate who spoke from the heart, and he was a man of peace. He was hated by the religious establishment of his day, and even by his own fellow Jews. Let me put a caveat on that: It was the pious Jewish leaders who didn't listen and turned others against him. "He who has ears, let him hear." The words he spoke were ones of direction, explanation, and mysteries that might not have been meant to be understood until this time period. He even said when asked by the disciples what things meant that it would be a mystery to a lot of people.

Since the finding of the Dead Sea Scrolls and the Nag Hammadi discoveries, books have been unearthed that lend a different slant to things. One that comes to mind is the Gospel of Thomas. These are just the condensed sayings of Christ or Yeshua without any religious dogma added. No dying on the cross for our sins, no explanation of anything that is associated with the dogma of today's Christian movement. No condemnation, guilt, control, or manipulative attempts. Now when you look at a distilled version of what he had to say in the scrolls of Thomas, along with other factors such as the Aramaic words he spoke, and examine the different, colorful, and beautiful meanings those have, you start to get a different picture. You start to get this picture of an enlightened master who was trying to show us things.

This brings up the questions of: Was he God's literal son? Was he divine? Was he an enlightened soul who had a purpose to fulfill? The gospels that we have in our Bibles today were manipulated into the Bible by Emperor Constantine around 325 A.D. at the Council of Nicaea. Evidently, Constantine wanted to reshape the movement that was born out of Christ for his own selfish purposes. Off of that, the church of Rome began to spin, along with all the hierarchical trappings and control of the people. It was all about control. The events that went on during this time are too extensive to go into, and there are much better books on this subject than I could write here. But the bottom line is that a lot of the books that could have been included in the Bible were discarded. Some of them from the Gnostic (*gnosis* meaning "knowledge" or "hidden knowledge") movement, which saw a much deeper meaning than what was written in the books Constantine included.

These books sometimes referred to things that Jesus implied—ideas like the kingdom of heaven being within us. Constantine couldn't use those books because if the kingdom was within, and God was within as Jesus said (quote: "I and the father are one."), then what would Constantine use to control the people? He wanted everything to be external. Obey the commandments or burn in Hell. Accept Christ as Savior or burn in Hell. Do what the church says. Feel guilt and fear, or God will punish you, and a whole host of things. Some of the gospels chosen could have even been manipulated to include dogma and may not have been written by Matthew or John or whomever. Most of them were written decades after Christ was gone.

So with all that being said (and check my facts, don't take my word for it), was Yeshua here for a different reason than we think? Was he here to point the way to what I call Transformation, Transcendence, and Truth? Think of the cross as a "T" and think of the three crosses on the hill as three "T"s—Transcendence, Transformation, and Truth. That came to me in a vision.

Now when you think about Christianity, many Christian churches and Christians don't represent these ideals and the ideals of the sayings of Christ and the actions of Christ. He said love thy neighbor, but they say let's go to war and kill. He said love thy enemies, but they say God's on our side. He said the kingdom of heaven is not over here or over there but something you can't see, and that the kingdom of heaven is within you. And they say you won't make it to the kingdom if you don't do this or do that, and that you will go to Hell or be destroyed! Christ said God was loving and merciful. They say God is angry, punishing, and sometimes even condones evil acts. Who would you rather believe? Is there any question?

Now you might say, why is Thunderhands talking about Christian things and not Native American beliefs? Well, you might be surprised to learn what some of the native beliefs are. They have many of the same concepts of another system that doesn't judge, Taoism, an Eastern viewpoint. And when you look at some of the enlightening things the Native American says or believes and the Taoist's philosophy, you find a close resemblance. And that is Nature with a capitol "N." You find sayings that are incredible and loving. One that comes to mind, and I am paraphrasing some of this: "You whites tend to believe that when man was created, Great Spirit breathed into him the breath of life, but we believe his breath took in all of nature as well." Well isn't that profound? The Tao oftentimes associates things with the elements of wood, wind, water, fire, etc. The Tao Te Ching speaks of water and nature and other natural elements like thunder and lightning. It's funny that Jesus called James and John "the sons of thunder." Jesus often spoke of crops and the wheat and fire. And he picked fishermen as some of his disciples. He walked on water and there were storms and lightning and thunder from the heavens. Open your eyes; Jesus' sayings were steeped in nature.

Thunder is big in Native American culture because it represents a shock, or waking up, or a cleansing and a calm after the storm. And so it is with the I-Ching. Thunderbeings are powerful beings featured on totem poles in the form of Thunderbirds. Drums are used in ceremony as ritualistic thunderous drums. The Lakota say that the first great mystery of the 16 great mysteries is the Sun, and everything was created from then on. Sometimes that sun is looked at as son or s-o-n, or Tunkashila. Many of the beliefs seem Eastern, and so many believe that the Native American came from the East over the land bridge that once existed up by the Aleutian Island Chain. And wasn't Yeshua Eastern or from the East? And where did he travel and what did he pick up during all those years that are missing in the Bible? It's funny that they are missing, isn't it? You would think that the Bible writers would have included that. I mean those are the informative years. It doesn't make sense, does it? It's like someone wanted to cut that part of the picture out. But you never know what's going to be found on the splicing room floor.

So does religion today espouse the real teachings of Christ, or are they in the same bag of trying to strike fear, condemnation, guilt, and control? Or maybe they want a lot of money when they pass the plate. Do they support the powers that be, along with war and hate? And do they stand idly by and watch the planet destroyed by greed, corruption, and war? And at times through history did they kill thousands in the name of Christ during the crusades? And how about the Inquisition, and burning people at the stake? What do you think Yeshua would say or think about that? Get behind me Satan! Why does the Church profile and hate certain groups of people as not worthy? Jesus hung out with prostitutes and tax collectors and those considered low-lifes.

Now I know there are a lot of sincere people who are Christians, and I am not here to judge anyone, or any system, because it's all an illusion anyway. But if you were to call anything the anti-Christ, it wouldn't be a person; it would be those who represented themselves as speaking for Christ, but then did just the opposite.

It's not about religion; it's about enlightenment. It's about love and all those who speak of love. It's about living in accordance with nature within yourself and without. It's not about four walls with a roof and steeple. It's about Grandmother Earth and Grandfather Sky and all of creation. Jesus spoke of wolves in sheep's clothing. He warned against being misled. Broad is the road to destruction, narrow the road to life. The Indians have a name for the good road; it is called the Red Road. Look what's being done to the planet today and to the people on it. Where is the love?

So the shift I am seeing that I mentioned at the beginning is a shift in consciousness about Christ or Jesus and religion. And I see a lot of people waking up. And a lot of people are writing books now about the lessons we can learn from Jesus' words and how to really understand what he was saying, and about how religion is a middleman that isn't needed. But if the consciousness shifts and people start connecting and loving one another, think of the possibilities. The government is sadly inadequate in spiritual matters. They are part of the problem, not the solution. They speak with a forked tongue, just like they did when they committed genocide on the original inhabitants of America. When the shift is complete they will either sink or swim. The politicians speak of God and Jesus out of one side of their mouths, and declare war out of the other. What have they really done for the homeless? Jesus spoke of the Good Samaritan. What about the elderly on fixed incomes? Need I go further? And that's just scratching the surface. Do you want to live in the kingdom that Yeshua spoke of? Then disavow all that you see around you. Be non-attached and go within. Ignore the duality so that you can change yourself inside and see that change take effect outside. As above, so below. Be a Christ, by using your Christ consciousness. Cast away all the negativity that you see around you in the media, the government, the schools, and religion. Be reborn, not born again. Pretty shocking, isn't it? But remember my name is Thunderhands, and thunder shocks and hands create by writing and by other means, like my drums. So maybe I'm beating a different kind of drum. Drums were used for communication. Do you know? Somebody has to speak from the heart, which also beats like a drum.

Speaking from the Heart

▼

INVARIABLY SOMETHING ARISES EVERY DAY that gives me pause to reflect on a certain situation about myself and others. I practice what I call "speaking from the heart." Sometimes it's with friends, other times with family. I get into trouble by doing this at times, unless the party I am talking to really understands what I am trying to say. With family you have to be careful, or so it seems, that things aren't taken the wrong way. I guess that's true with anybody, for that matter. I won't go into personal details, but when you speak from the heart you have a tendency not to hold things back.

Sometimes people take what you say to their heart and everything is OK. If what you say hurts someone or strikes a chord they don't like, it can cause separation for a period of time. In certain cases what you are saying may be to purge what is perceived by one's self as trauma or feelings that need to be vented in the spirit of healing. I always try to preface comments with a thought that indicates that I am speaking for the good of everyone involved. If done correctly a healing can take place on certain levels. It's a touchy thing, because often what you mean to say can be diluted or distorted by the fact that words don't always convey the meaning you intended. It's like that saying: "Words are but crumbs from the feast of the mind." I have had situations when talking with family where things are perceived as coming from a place of ego or manipulation, when in fact that wasn't the case at all. It's hard to tell how people will take things because we are all so different, and we all have that ego that has its own agenda. At times I have had my own immediate family disown or distance themselves from me and the things I intended to convey. With my siblings it could be a perception formed from child-hood, that one person was favored over another by the parents who raised us, when in fact that might not be true. Social conditioning and parenting play a big part in our lives. Egos feel threatened, particularly regarding matters of spirit and spirituality. I think the key to understanding one another is to take it in the spirit it was meant. I always leave the door open for discussion after a conversation with friends and family. Because no matter how good our intention, we might not have conveyed our feelings in a fashion that didn't "tread on the tail of the tiger" (I-Ching).

I would like to think that dialog will somehow overcome any misun-derstandings. Also, I have found that everything will be fine until a third party gets involved who has no idea of the relationship that you have established between the person you intended to communicate certain things to and yourself. It's all a growth process. One of the greatest and wisest men of all time, Jesus, or Yeshua, was misunder-stood by many to the point of his death. Sometimes he said or did things that he felt needed to be conveyed for a healing to take place. I like the spirit of the saying, "Never let the sun set until that feeling of anger or misunderstanding can be dispersed." We are all here for a certain period of time. We don't know from one day to the next how long that will be. But certainly we wouldn't want a division or hard feelings to exist for too long because of this very simple fact. Impermanence is part of life, so let's try to be at peace with all of our brothers and sisters on the planet. This includes everyone, and not just immediate family. When I use the term immediate, I mean related by blood. However, even that term can cause division because we are all family. We are all one, connected by Great Spirit, or the Tao. Maybe the reason misunderstandings occur is that this fact isn't realized. We are a mirror of ourselves. So when someone speaks to us and it strikes a chord, maybe we shouldn't make it good or bad. It's just a learning process. Like I said earlier, we can bypass the duality and look at the big picture. Acceptance, understanding, love, and at the same time, detachment. Great Spirit often uses us in ways that can't always be comprehended at the time. So reflect or contemplate on what others may be conveying, because it's like we are talking to ourselves. It's the spirit of the law, not the law. Nobody is more holy than the other, but we can give credit where credit is due. And that's to the higher power, or the Tao, for guiding us in whatever way it uses to manifest the lessons we or others learn in life. Don't just see what you want to see through the eyes of your conditioning. Look beyond that and find the pearls of wisdom being conveyed through that source.

Buddha and Christ Mind

WHEN YOU SAY A PRAYER or make supplication to the deity, there are certain things you should remember. Remember that your essence or spirit is actually the Christ or Buddha within. That's why in Zen they say "Buddha mind" or "Christ mind," if you will, because that very same spirit is within you or *is* you. Through years of conditioning we forget who we are. We become accustomed to thinking that our ego is us, when in reality our "essence" is the true self or the true mind. That's why when some bow to the Buddha or make supplication to Christ it is really what that image represents that we are paying homage to. That image represents what our true capability is. It's a reminder to us. Meditation or just being still is the only approach that allows us to see the thoughts and habits that get in the way of that clear being or essence within. To catch a glimpse is to be inspired. Little glimpses over time allow us to see longer ones. This is the way to walk the path and allow that essence or light to come through. Be as a child again, have the innocence of a child, and you will regain your true heritage which is Buddha mind or Christ mind.

Reverence

▼

THE DICTIONARY DEFINES REVERENCE as a feeling or attitude of deep respect tinged with awe or veneration. Where is the reverence today? Reverence is like a prayer, but it's more. It's having respect and honor for whatever you are contemplating or coming into contact with. Let's look at several examples. First let's take food. The food we eat every day. Do we just cook it, or order it from a restaurant and then proceed to cram it in our mouths without thinking about or having reverence for it? Now you might say a prayer like "Thank you Creator for this food you provide," and that's a good start, but many people don't even do that. Reverence is different. Reverence is thinking, or contemplation of where this food came from and how it got to you. It's not like it just appeared; it came from Grandmother Earth. You might look at the rice on your plate and not think too much about it. Let's think about the word "humility" in regards to the rice. It wouldn't be in front of you if there wasn't humility involved. How is humility involved? Planting, cultivation, and harvest. Do you think this is easy? The growing of rice involves many things before it gets to our plate. It involves care, planning, and working with the elements to grow it. It involves one of our relations getting down in the mud on their hands and knees to plant a seed or sprout, and space it carefully apart. It means looking at the seasons and the best time to plant and working with the elements of Mother Earth. It means acceptance of accidents and

we realize that everything that we have, even that keyboard, comes from the universal source? Reverence for all things. Being thankful on a higher level means more than just saying a repetitive prayer of words or sounds without feeling them. Reverence comes from the heart, not the head. Reverence is a feeling. Feelings from the heart empower us. Some say that when you feel things from the heart and visualize them, it empowers you to create within the divine web of the universe or the source of all things. Now let's address reverence for our fellow man, our fellow beings on the planet. Do we look at one race as inferior to the next? Do we look at a person's skin color and see it as beautiful? Do we look at the shape of a person's eyes and the eyes themselves as something deep, beautiful, and part of the great mystery? How about the way we treat our fellow man? Is it with reverence and the understanding that no one person is above another? We are all equal in the natural order. Having a lot of money or prestige or being famous doesn't change this fact. The more we look at people and how they function the more we see spirit at work in all of us. We can do wonderful things for our relations or we can do "un-reverential" things. We can be bigoted and hateful. We can think of another race as being savage or backward. Is a race savage because it lives next to nature or closer to the earth? No! The ones who are savage are the ones that have no reverence for things of nature and want to possess or control things as objects. They look at land and our natural resources with greed and as something to own. No one owns the earth; it is for all our relations and should be shared, not hoarded. Some even justify the taking of a human life for this greed. When they do that they "take all that person ever could have been." They can never take what he was, because their spirit and memory lives on in the hearts of people. How about killing animals for food, or plants for that matter. Is it OK? I would say yes, because it is meant that we live. But we must thank the animal or plant for giving its spirit so that it may live on in us. Do we do that? Do the mass killings at slaughter houses do that? No! But if we eat any meat we can still have reverence and thank the animal right then and there for giving its spirit so that it may live on in us. So how will this attitude of reverence affect you? It will affect not only you but the whole planet, for every reverential thought will help all. It is healing for yourself and others to do this, because then life becomes "Good Medicine," or something that is healing for all and the planet. Plants can feel and think; they are intelligent. Plants and herbs and food can bring a healing balanced quality to your life if viewed in the right manner. Think of how the world would change if we all were reverential to everything. This is true love, for reverence must come from the heart. Try this in your life. Don't expect it to take hold right away, because we are all conditioned in this fast-paced society. Don't be hard on yourself for not remembering all the time, but give love to yourself when you do remember. Pretty soon it feels good getting all that love and giving it, too. This is what will change you and the planet. This is what will change your heart and make it open instead of closed. Other people will pick up on it and be naturally attracted to your energy and it will rub off. They will think or feel that here is a real person of the earth, someone who cares and loves. Blessings and reverence to you all.

The Tree

▼

A TREE DOES NOT WAKE UP in the morning with any agenda or compulsion. It does not think about work, sex, routine, and mortality. Its roots sink into Mother Earth for nourishment, and its branches and leaves receive from Grandfather sky. It cares not if there is a storm in its life because it is flexible and bends with the wind. It lives through many seasons because it is firmly rooted. A tree is intelligent but does not worry or think; it just is, and is part of the universal knowing. It does not have an ego, so there are no blocks to receiving or being one with the universe or Tao. Some trees are 2,000 years old and still going strong. Be like a tree, and if you have a hard time with that, go ask one to mentor you, heal you, share its energy with you.

The Family

▼

THE ANCIENT CHINESE HAD a concept of order in the family where each person had a respective place and duty to the other. The family was an integral unit of support for each other. The bond was close and reverence was of the highest order. The particulars can be found in the I-Ching, or Book of Changes, under hexagram 37. This hexagram can and was easily applied to society at large, and also to order within oneself. The overall picture, though, is that of people working together in the proper manner. Most people and societies have little use for this concept now, as they have little use for the old ways in Native people's culture. Respect and reverence seem to be missing, as are loyalty and love! When the family breaks down, so goes society, and when society breaks down, so goes family! Some of you have lost connections with, or have just lost family. But we are all family in a sense, and voids can be filled with our sense of love to those who need it. Fulfill their loss.

Don't Give Away
Your Power

▼

THE POWERS THAT BE and the governments are not your friends, they are your enemies! They have manipulated you into giving your power away through self-indulgence and addiction to a dysfunctional, self-destructive system. They have turned you against one another by creating a two-party political system that does nothing but cause animosity and a illusion that one side can fix all that is wrong! You have become addicted (their game plan) to all that is mundane, from the latest technology and entertainment (games) to a whole gamut of illusions. These would be: financial security, personal security from supposed threats, medical security, food production, and social security. "The American dream?" Money is printed on pieces of paper that have nothing to back it up! The powers that be (money people) run the governments and have an agenda to make mass slaves of you all and to live off your hard labor, like a forced labor camp. People are like lemmings speeding to work back and forth on the freeway every day in a crazed ritual that gets them nowhere, when they should be living off the land! The elite money people rule! Their agenda is falling apart, because the wolves are at the people's door, and natural disasters are breaking their already broken budget! But they really don't care!! Their next move to protect their assets (Plan B) will be drastic and shocking.

How long will you stand by while they play their rigged game! They probably have silently killed more people than all the wars put together through starvation, mismanaged healthcare, covert operations, and neglect of their promises! These people are the personification of evil and they speak with a forked tongue. They take advantage of your trust and good heart! Get ready to be self-sufficient, live off the land, and to protect yourselves. Get ready to help those who are older or infirm to do likewise. You can't count on them when the chips are down! Forget politics and governments. Be self-sufficient. Don't be grist for the mill. Band together, think coherently, and have council with one another. Now! Before it's too late! Before it all breaks down and they go to Plan B! Maybe Plan B is already starting. Is that shocking? You bet!

A Tracker's Point of View

▼

HAVE YOU EVER TRACKED an animal? How about a person? Everything leaves a special imprint and energy, even after they have left the scene! I am not fond of imprints in an urban setting or the city. It's a massive chaotic jumble of energy with vibes bouncing everywhere! In the city you can't really hear nature. It is for the most part obliterated by the sounds of heavy machinery. Buses, trucks, and cars spew their noise and exhaust. People talk louder or scream to each other on their cell phones. There is always a siren from a police car or ambulance. Then you have the car alarms, the "beep beep" sounds from trucks backing up, the gardeners with their blowing dirt machines, and the people who drive by in their cars with music so loud you can hear it a block away! The "tracks" on the sidewalk level and bus stops are so disgusting I'll spare you the details! No wonder everyone is anxious and neurotic!

Contrast that with walking in a wilderness area. You can hear a leaf drop if you're still enough and tuned in. You can hear a twig snap and a small animal scramble in the bushes. You feel and hear the wind blowing in the trees and a myriad of birds talking to you and other animals. A hawk may fly overhead and screech out a mating call. You might hear the trickle of a stream or babbling brook! Your smell picks up on wildflowers and surrounding earth aromas! All the bushes, trees, and shrubs grow wild and free instead of being trimmed, cut down, and butchered. The circle of life is alive and well out in the wilderness! I have just scratched the surface regarding what is and what should be. This is why I don't get too upset when I see the forces of nature come down and wreak what some call havoc, wiping some of this stuff clean and off the face of the earth. When you think about the havoc and chaos man creates every day, then what nature does seems appropriate and kind! I wonder what would happened if we went around chanting in a barely audible voice phrases like "Birds singing," "Wind blowing in the trees," "Rain falling from the sky," "Water flowing." Maybe we should try it and see. A continual prayer if you will! Words can be good medicine and a strong force for your thoughts to form around.

Hopi Prophecy Revisited

▼

A GLIMPSE INTO CERTAIN SEGMENTS of Hopi prophecy are very interesting! As I say in my book *Emergence*, "Thunder looks at things in a metaphorical fashion sometimes!" Not everything is as it seems to be on the face of it! You have to look at the spirit behind the words! The only concise knowledge we have from the inside seems to be from the Hopi elders themselves, as related to a man named Frank Waters in his excellent book. This book was written in 1963, however, and some of the terms used may need to be updated. The term World War III seems inappropriate now because the whole world is at war already. There are wars going on everywhere! World War III is here! The statement that it would be started by "those people who brought the first light," might need to be seen with different eyes! This was always thought to mean people from the East and some type of enlightenment, but could it mean the United States and the creation of atomic weaponry, i.e., "first light of destruction"? The fact that the United States (or world?) could be destroyed by radioactivity or some type of nuclear reaction is now, in my opinion, leaning more towards radioactivity in general!

Further consideration on the commentary offers this: "Those who take no part in the making of world division by ideology accept that all races: Black, White, Red, and Yellow, are brothers in being." They are the ones on the right road, as stated in the prophecy, and are "keepers." Another true statement is, "The war will be a spiritual conflict with material matters." Oh how true that is! Something else that rings true is that the emergence into the fifth world has begun and is being made by "the humble people of little nations, tribes, and racial minorities." Mention is made of seeds in different contexts. The seeds could be us, or wisdom keepers, planted here a long time ago by the star people, or seeds from previous worlds (dimensions?) springing up or appearing, planted in our hearts in this dimensional reality through our ancestors the star people! These are mentioned as being the same, depending on how you look at it. These seeds play a big part of emergence into the fifth world. The I-Ching (Chinese Book of Changes) depicts a seed as a new beginning, or a sprout pushing up through the earth from below. The Hopi emerged through the sipapus from below. The more I pray and ponder on these matters the more I see! Perhaps I shall ponder and pray further. Something to consider in these chaotic times!

Where is Your Heart?

ARE NATURAL DISASTERS natural occurrences that result in disastrous consequences? First of all, let me say that I have compassion for anyone who has had to endure the wake-up call of a sudden and powerful natural occurrence! Sometimes I see the comments people put up after weather news articles that I read, and they completely destroy my faith in my fellow man. Just when I think people are waking up! I will read an article, for instance, on the floods in North Korea, and the suffering there, and some ignorant person from America will post a comment indicating that those (racial slur) people get what they deserve and should be wiped off the face of the earth, blah, blah, blah! Well I tell you what, when it hits them, as it soon will according to Hopi and other prophecies, they will be singing a different tune! Personally I can't wait for Mother Nature to reclaim the concrete jungles of the vast wasteland of city blight in America. It would be a wonderful thing to see trees, flowers, and plants growing up through the concrete of the urban self-created disaster! I hope it happens even if I don't make it through the natural occurrence. Then all those hate-mongering people who point their fingers at other countries or races will have to try, and I emphasize *try,* to survive off the land! Good luck, Sport! Most people would have no idea what to do if the supermarket shelves were suddenly bare or the water quit running from the tap. Most people take these things for granted and assume it could never happen here. Do you know how

long you can survive without water? Three days! Would you know
how to get water if that scenario were to play out? Old trackers
and naturalists know. Even if it were in the city they know how to
survive off condensation and other means. Most people would be in
a big panic and would resort to stealing and looting. Water would be
like gold. Food would be scarce or non-existent. Think what would
happen if the two major rail lines went down, or if the main aque-
ducts supplying water to a city stopped pumping water. Don't take
what Grandmother Earth supplies to us for granted, and don't laugh
at other people's misfortune. When push comes to shove it can and
probably will happen at any given moment in a neighborhood near
you. So again I say, where is your heart, Kola!?

Kokopelli!!

▼

WHO IS THE WORLD-FAMOUS humpbacked flute player, sower of seeds, bringer of rain, and ancient "wuya," or deity of fertility? His importance is beyond our knowing! The hump on his back is sometimes thought to be a sack! In it are seeds of maize and other good things, mystical things, Shamanistic things! Or maybe it represents the seeding of mankind by the star people. His music is mesmerizing and overpowering. There are literally thousands of pictographs and petrographic paintings of him on rocks spread everywhere in the Americas! He sometimes is depicted with an extended phallus because of the strength of his power to cause fertility in all things! Sometimes he is shown having intercourse with maidens or flying above animals or near a cloud (bringer of rain), or snake! He is everywhere! He carries a walking stick or curved staff with a hook on the end! The sweet sound of his flute or presence will not be ignored! He is a mystery as much as anything can be! He is the ancient of the ancients in the land of the pueblo people, which extends north to south, east to west! He is sometimes depicted as a wanderer who could arrive at any moment in any disguise! Sometimes he will take on the image of an insect or an anthropomorphic character! His instrument, the flute, is the oldest known instrument to man! Honor and reverence is in order for Kokopelli! Never underestimate the power of the humpbacked, flute-carrying flirt! I also am a flute player, so of course he is my hero!

The Closing and the Opening

▼

SINCE I BEGAN SETTING DOWN the thoughts for this book, many events have occurred both in the world and my personal consciousness. Events that I suspected would happened have happened. The world and planet seem to be going through changes at a very rapid pace. All I know is what I can perceive with my senses, including the gift of a sixth sense, or what I call a "knowing." Many believe that a certain calendar date as set forth by the Mayan culture may be very significant. I will leave that to the Mayans and the passing of time. Some say cyclical events are in play and possible manipulation by outside forces beyond our dimension is imminent. Some say not to worry because it's Grandmother Earth taking care of herself. There are the doomsday evangelists who say the end of the world is near, while others are completely oblivious to the energy or events surrounding us and go on with their lives in a day-to-day carefree way, with a "devil may care" attitude. Some people think that technology is a boon and will cure all our ills. Now we come to what I perceive and, I might add, what other Wisdom Keepers see or feel also. I choose few things as my lode star. One would be that I choose to walk the middle path of balance. The other "compass headings" would be to continue going with my higher self, with my glass always half full and ready to receive.

The main body or preceding thoughts in this work I believe are timeless and entertaining, while at the same time possessing a deeper mystical meaning. Obviously they were meant to help you on your path and offer guidance from a channeled, higher, or different way of thinking. But the questions that could possibly arise are: "Well what do I do now?" or "What can I expect in the future?" or "How do I walk the Red Road?" (or, as the Taoists say, the "path.") The best answer to those questions is to just keep walking. But there is a caveat to walking. In order to stay centered and balanced or on the right path it is essential that we not walk blindly. In my second book, which is a novel called *Emergence,* I talk about The Keepers and The Sleepers." The Keepers are the ones who are awake or have been awakened to, at the very least, survival, and at the very most, waking up to help others who might be blind or sleepwalking through life. I call these people The Sleepers.

Let's look at the current situation, which may very well have to do with the survival aspect of walking. Even though some people think that the changes on the earth and in this illusion we call a world are cyclical, the fact remains that they are happening... things such as unprecedented and record-breaking storms and curious weather patterns. Geological events such as earthquakes, volcanoes, and the beginning of a magnetic pole shift are happening. In space we have asteroids passing by in close proximity to earth, and scientists at NASA are saying to expect a solar storm. The solar storm is in the first stages and will only get stronger. It will very likely take out most satellites and communication grids around the earth for a possible ten years. This in itself would trigger cataclysmic events spoken of by credible experts in the field. The grids and electricity, along with computers, control all the companies, systems, networks, and supply chains that allow us to exist. This would include water, electricity, food control, transportation, and other essential services. The effect would be a return to the basics of survival provided by Mother Earth, which we are not only out of tune with, but destroying. As I write these words governments are talking about major climate changes, trying to figure out what to do about them and the effect of these changes on our farming. These changes are happening so fast and are so unprecedented that they are having summits on the topic. These summits are just talk and are coming up with no meaningful answers. Our planet will have 7 billion people on it by October 31, 2011, just days from this writing. More people, less food. Most experts say this is a recipe for disaster. Although the politicians and others who are in control carry on as if these things can be fixed, the consensus among some is that this started a long time ago, and is so far along that it can't be fixed. You might use the analogy of the little Dutch boy sticking his finger in the dike.

Let's talk about the economic situation. As I write this, there are so many things happening on that level it would make a grown man cry! I am not an economist, but I don't need to be. All I need to do is look around at what's happening. Most of the American states are either broke or are having a major budgets crisis. American and European economies are going "belly up" and the effect on the majority of the population has created an emergency mode. The elderly, veterans, and homeless are suffering severely from a lack of care and services, programs are being cut, and if you look closely it's so bad it wouldn't be overkill to say it's almost like a twisted geno-cide. As I write these words groups are forming around the world, with origins in America, that are demonstrating against poverty and an elitist society where the rich and powerful are the one percent and the poor are the 99%, to quote their slogan. It seems like we have a powder keg situation where one spark could cause the whole thing to blow.

Most societies in the past (well documented) have fallen because of depleting resources, overpopulation, mismanagement, and war. The societies that fell were the Mayans, the Anasazi, and others. All the earmarks of what caused them to fall are now befalling not just one society, but the whole earth. The real kicker is that the whole earth is one big society now because of technology, so if it's going to go down or fall, it will be worldwide and not isolated. I'm wondering at this point if most people "get the drift" here.

This could be a closing and a beginning of what we conceive of as business as usual. I might pose some questions at this point. Are we so far along in the process of decline that it is irreversible and will just have to run its course? If this is the case, are you as a person and/or family ready for the events that seem imminent as you walk this journey of life? If you want to talk about blame, there is plenty to go around, including everyone on the planet who was and is sleepwalking through all of this.

So what is the answer to the predicament we find ourselves in? Most ancient civilizations, including the Hopi, say we originated from the stars or star brothers and thus we shall return. Or maybe they will return, or already have. There are many theories regarding this, but one thing is for sure. The government wishes to hide any and all information regarding any life, technology, and truth about life beyond what we perceive. I have a knowing that this won't last for long. Those of us who have experienced different dimensions know where and how certain things happen in this illusion we call reality. Our Hopi, Zuni, and Navajo brothers know, as do many who care to open up to higher thought and direction.

I have a term that I have used, or a drum I beat, time and time again, and that is this: "It's all about energy." A major component of this thought is "vibratory levels." Is this something new? It may be new to you, but the ancients have known for quite some time. It has been revealed to me and others as well. One only need look at history and the so-called esoteric beliefs of the wise ones or wisdom-keepers of this and earlier civilizations. Eisenstein touched on it, and cutting-edge physicists are beginning to discover the bridge between what most consider as science fiction with that of fact. What was thought of as other-worldly or out of the question is coming into focus as entirely plausible. For instance, who would have thought as few as five decades ago that we would be seeing the incredible leap in what we call technology that we see now? As a fully rated pilot, among other things, I can tell you that what we are seeing now is off the charts. Things like small electronic devices the size of a thin wafer can hold gigabytes of information such as sound recordings. We have jumped from having recording disks or records that could hold eight sound recordings at the most to a small device that can hold hundreds if not thousands of songs or sound recordings inside a piece of "electronic plastic" no bigger than a few inches long and less than an eighth of an inch thick. We have aircraft that travel at warp speed through the atmosphere, communication on invisible sound frequencies, including images that circle the globe in seconds.

If we know about these things, think of what we don't know about what the "powers that be" are keeping hidden. I'm just scratching the surface here, as you all know.

But let's get back to "its all about energy." The truth is that anything we can see in this realm and outside this realm is made up of energy and vibrates at certain frequencies. Do you think for one minute that the minds that conceived the technological inventions don't far surpass anything we can, quote, "see"? If you don't think so, think again. The ancient avatars whom we have deified have not only mentioned the capabilities we all have as humans, but have even given us techniques to access our own "hidden knowledge." If you're not sleep-walking in this life then you have become aware or enlightened to these facts. We supposedly ordinary people have powers that can boggle the mind. Do you think you need what physicists and scientists call a "worm-hole in space" to access other dimensions? The string theory posited by cutting-edge thought says there are as many as 15 or more dimensions. I believe, and will even say I know, that these dimensions can be accessed by raising the vibratory level surrounding and within us. This would again be called an energy field, or a personal energy field. How do you think shamans, holy men, yogis, medicine men and others perform what some would call miraculous feats and even healings? Some are "gifted" with this spiritual knowledge, while others are using spiritual disciplines passed down through the centuries.

The point is, the answers to many of the problems we face lie within. The answers we seek are available, not out there, but inside of you. Nobody can do the work for you. You must make the effort yourself!

The first step is listening: listening to the wind, or listening for that higher direction and realizing that it is there. Then comes speaking from the heart and sharing it with others. I can't give you a crash course in consciousness raising or becoming aware, but maybe my writings, along with those of others who are directing, will help. I can't save the world or you; but you can realize, and in realization there is an opening. In my book *Emergence* I describe ancient techniques that I think will help, so I won't repeat them here. These techniques can be found in many ancient traditions and disciplines also, so I don't have a corner on the market, so to speak. Just the fact that you picked up this book and are reading it is a step in the right direction. There is a certain spirit that permeates this book and just having it could make a difference. Edgar Cayce, the famous modern-day prophet, would sleep with a book under his pillow and absorb the energy and knowledge from it. Sometimes it would raise his vibratory level. We do have an energy field around us called an aura that is very adept at absorbing things that will benefit us. Some call raising your vibratory level, "lifting the spirit." So with that thought in mind, and considering what we see in the illusive reality around us, don't rule anything out. Wake up to a new way of thinking and let go of the old. You might call it both a closing and an opening.

Blessings to all my relations (Mitakuye Oyasin)
Roger Thunderhands

Glossary

Apache: Apache is the collective term for several culturally related groups of Native Americans in the United States originally from the Southwest United States. These indigenous peoples of North America speak a Southern Athabaskan (Apachean) language which is related linguistically to the languages of Athabaskan speakers of Alaska and western Canada. The modern term Apache excludes the related Navajo people. Since the Navajo and the other Apache groups are clearly related through culture and language, they are all considered Apachean. Apachean peoples formerly ranged over eastern Arizona, northwestern Mexico, New Mexico, Texas, and the southern Great Plains.

Apostate: Apostasy, defection or revolt from, "away, apart." It is the formal disaffiliation from, abandonment, or renunciation of a religion by a person. One who commits apostasy, apostatizes, and is an apostate. These terms have a pejorative implication in everyday use. The term is used by sociologists to mean renunciation and criticism of, or opposition to, a person's former religion, in a technical sense and without pejorative connotation. The term is sometimes also used by extension to refer to renunciation of a non-religious belief or cause, such as a political party, brain trust, or, facetiously, a sports team. Apostasy is generally not a self-definition and very few former believers call themselves apostates because of the pejorative implications of the term. Many religious movements consider it a vice (sin), a corruption of the virtue of piety, in the sense that when piety fails, apostasy is the result. Many religious groups and some states punish apostates. Apostates may be shunned by the members of their former religious group or subjected to formal or informal punishment. This may be the official policy of the religious group or may be the action of its members. A Christian church may in certain circumstances excommunicate the apostate, while some Islamic scriptures demand the death penalty for apostates. The death penalty is still applied to apostates by some Muslim states, but not in Christianity or Judaism.

Aramaic: Aramaic is a group of languages belonging to the Afroasiatic language phylum. The name of the language is based on the name of Aram, an ancient region in central Syria. Within this family, Aramaic belongs to the Semitic family, and more specifically, is a part of the Northwest Semitic subfamily, which also includes Canaanite languages such as Hebrew and Phoenician. Aramaic script was widely adopted for other languages and is ancestral to both the Arabic and modern Hebrew alphabets. During its 3,000-year written history, Aramaic has served variously as a language of administration of empires and as a language of divine worship. It was the day-to-day language of Israel in the Second Temple period (539 BCE – 70 CE), was the language spoken by Jesus, is the language of large sections of the biblical books of Daniel and Ezra, and is the main language of the Talmud.

Bad Medicine: Would be the opposite of Good Medicine (see Good Medicine) and would be an event that would be looked upon as non-beneficial, not good, or a bad omen!

Black Elk: He aka Sapa (Black Elk) (December 1863 – August 19, 1950) was a famous Wichasa Wakán (Medicine Man or Holy Man) of the Oglala Lakota (Sioux). He was a Heyoka and a second cousin of Crazy Horse.

Breech Cloth: A breech cloth, or breech clout, is a form of loincloth consisting of a strip of material (usually a narrow rectangle) passed between the thighs and held up in front and behind by a belt or string. Often, the flaps hang down in front and back. In most Native American tribes, men used to wear some form of breech cloth, often with leggings. The style differed from tribe to tribe. In many tribes, the flaps hung down in front and back; in others, the breech cloth looped outside of the belt and was tucked into the inside, for a more fitted look. Sometimes the breech cloth was much shorter and a decorated apron panel was attached in front and behind. A Native American woman or teenage girl might also wear a fitted breech cloth underneath her skirt, but not as outerwear. However, in many tribes young girls did wear breech cloths like the boys until they became old enough for skirts and dresses.

Buddha: Siddhartha Gautama was a spiritual teacher on the Indian subcontinent, on whose teachings Buddhism was founded. In most Buddhist traditions, he is regarded as the Supreme Buddha of our age, "Buddha" meaning "awakened one" or "the enlightened one." The time of his birth and death are uncertain. Most early 20th-century historians dated his lifetime as c. 563 BCE to 483

BCE, but more recent opinion dates his death to between 486 and 483 BCE, or, according to some, between 411 and 400 BCE. By tradition, Gautama is said to have been born in the small state of Kapilavastu, in what is now Nepal, and later to have taught primarily throughout regions of eastern India such as Magadha and Kosala. Gautama, also known as Sakyamuni ("Sage of the Sakyas"), is the primary figure in Buddhism, and accounts of his life, discourses, and monastic rules are believed by Buddhists to have been summarized after his death and memorized by his followers. Various collections of teachings attributed to him were passed down by oral tradition, and first committed to writing about 400 years later.

Cabala: The Cabala or Kabala is a set of esoteric teachings meant to explain the relationship between an eternal and mysterious Creator and the mortal and finite universe (His creation). While it is heavily used by some denominations, it is not a denomination in and of itself; it is a set of scriptures that exist outside the traditional Jewish scriptures. Cabala seeks to define the nature of the universe and the human being, the nature and purpose of existence, and various other ontological questions. It also presents methods to aid understanding of these concepts and to thereby attain spiritual realization.

Chi: See **Energy**.

Constantine, Emperor: Constantine the Great (Latin: Flavius Valerius Aurelius Constantinus Augustus; 27 February 272 – 22 May 337), also known as Constantine I or Saint Constantine, was Roman Emperor from 306 to 337. Well known for being the first Roman emperor to convert to Christianity, Constantine and co-Emperor Licinius issued the Edict of Milan in 313, which proclaimed religious tolerance of all religions throughout the empire. Constantine built a new imperial residence in place of Byzantium, naming it Constantinople, which would later be the capital of the Eastern Roman Empire for over one thousand years. He is thought of as the founder of the Eastern Roman Empire.

Cyclical: A process that returns to its beginning and repeats itself in the same sequence. Such processes are seen in many fields, such as physics, mathematics, biology, astronomy, economics, audio frequency, etc.

Dogma: Dogma is the established belief or doctrine held by a religion, or by extension, by some other group or organization. It is authoritative and not to be disputed, doubted, or diverged from by the practitioners or believers. The term derives from Greek, and means "that which seems to one, opinion or belief" and "to think, to suppose, to imagine." By the first century dogma came to signify laws or ordinances adjudged and imposed upon others. The plural is either dogmas or dogmata. Today, it is sometimes used as a synonym for systematic theology.

Drum circle: A Drum circle consists of several drummers using various types of drums and percussion instruments in unison to create a tribal type rhythm in which members entrain themselves with each other. Sometimes drum circles will be used for healing, communicating, and relating or becoming one in a spiritual sense. Drums have been used since the dawn of man to practice ritual and ceremony and are one of the oldest instruments on earth, only predated by the flute.

Drum and rattle: The drum and rattle are instruments used in Native American and other indigenous people's culture to contact Great Spirit, perform healing ceremonies, and dance to summon spirits. The rattles and drums are usually made by an elder or medicine man or woman.

Duality, or Dualism: From the Latin word *duo*, meaning "two," denotes a state of two parts. The term "dualism" was originally coined to denote co-eternal binary opposition, a meaning that is preserved in metaphysical and philosophical duality discourse but has been diluted in general or common usages. Dualism can refer to moral dualism, (e.g., the conflict between good and evil), mind-body or mind-matter dualism (e.g., Cartesian Dualism), or physical and spiritual dualism (e.g., the Chinese Yin and Yang).

Ecological: Ecology is the scientific study of the relations that living organisms have with respect to each other and their natural environment. Variables of interest to ecologists include the composition, distribution, amount (biomass), number, and changing states of organisms within and among ecosystems. Ecosystems are hierarchical systems that are organized into a graded series of regularly interacting and semi-independent parts (e.g., species) that aggregate into higher orders of complex integrated wholes (e.g., communities).

Edgar Cayce: Edgar Cayce (1877–1945) was an American psychic who allegedly had the ability to give answers to questions on subjects such as healing or Atlantis while in a hypnotic trance. Though Cayce himself was a devout Christian and lived before the emergence of the New Age Movement, some believe he was the founder of the movement and influenced its teachings. Cayce became a celebrity toward the end of his life and the publicity given to his prophecies has over-shadowed what to him were usually considered the more important parts of his work, such as healing (the vast majority of his readings were given for people who were sick) and theology (Cayce was a lifelong, devout member of the Disciples of Christ). Today there are thousands of Cayce students and more than 300 books written about Edgar Cayce. Members of Cayce's organization, the Association for Research and Enlightenment (A.R.E.) exist worldwide and Edgar Cayce Centers are found in more than 35 countries.

Energy, or Spiritual Energy: In traditional Chinese culture, qi (also chi or ch'i) is an active principle forming part of any living thing. Qi is frequently translated as life energy, life force, or energy flow. Qi is the central underlying principle in traditional Chinese medicine and martial arts. The literal translation of qi is breath, air, or gas. The Hindu equivalent would be the term "prana."

Essence: The essence of a person might best be described in terms of the unpolluted or childlike mind. A mind that has not yet been conditioned by the norms of society, parents, schools, religions, and other institutions. It can also be thought of as the part of one's being that is closest to God, the source, the Tao, Great Spirit or whatever term one wishes to use. See also: Higher self.

Feng shui: Feng shui is an ancient Chinese system of geomancy believed to use the laws of both Heaven (Chinese astronomy) and Earth to help one improve life by receiving positive "Chi." The term feng shui literally translates as "wind-water" in English. Historically, feng shui was widely used to orient buildings, often spiritually significant structures such as tombs, but also dwellings and other structures, in an auspicious manner. Depending on the particular style of feng shui being used, an auspicious site could be determined by reference to local features such as bodies of water, stars, or a compass. Feng shui was suppressed in China during the cultural revolution in the 1960s, but has since seen an increase in popularity.

Gi: A Lakota people's term for the third cardinal point of the east and represents the rising sun, clarity, and enlightenment. It is represented by the color yellow.

Give-away: Give-aways can be traced back to the tribes of the midwestern and high plains. In the broad sense, a give-away is nearly the reverse of today's modern culture's understanding of gift-giving. In the majority culture, the expectation is to receive gifts when being honored, recognized, or celebrated on special occasions, such as birthdays, graduations, etc. Historically, in the Native American tradition, many tribes have conducted a give-away out of a sense of honor. One gives to strangers, not simply hoping to make friends, but because it is the honorable thing to do. One gives to honor a relative, and this in turn honors that person in the eyes of the community. One gives when one seemingly has nothing to give. One gives to others who are in need. In many Native American cultures, what matters is not what someone has, but what the person is able to give away to others. It is not the value of the gift, but the giving itself that is culturally relevant. Giving a gift that may not have significant monetary worth, but significant spiritual or personal value, is a sign of a giving heart.

Gnostic: Gnosticism (from *gnostikos*, "learned," from Greek: *gnosis*, knowledge) is a scholarly term for a set of religious beliefs and spiritual practices common to early Christianity, Hellenistic Judaism, Greco-Roman mystery religions, Zoroastrianism (especially Zurvanism), and Neoplatonism. A common characteristic of some of these groups was the teaching that the realization of Gnosis (esoteric or intuitive knowledge), is the way to salvation of the soul from the material world. Jesus is identified by some Gnostic sects as an embodiment of the supreme being who became incarnate to bring gnosis to the earth. Others adamantly deny that the supreme being came in the flesh, claiming Jesus to be merely a human who attained divinity through gnosis and taught his disciples to do the same.

Good Medicine: A tribal term which in simple terms means an event in your life, or in life in general, that is good, beneficial, or a positive omen.

Gospel of Thomas: The Gospel According to Thomas, commonly shortened to the Gospel of Thomas, is a well preserved early Christian, non-canonical sayings-gospel discovered near Nag Hammadi, Egypt, in December 1945, in one of a group of books known as the Nag Hammadi library. The Gospel of Thomas was found among a collection of fifty-two writings that included, in addition to an excerpt from Plato's Republic, gospels claiming to have been written by Jesus' disciple Philip. Scholars have speculated that the works were buried in response to a letter from the bishop Athanasius, who for the first time declared a strict canon of Christian scripture. The Coptic language text, the second of seven contained in what modern-day scholars have designated as Codex II, is composed of 114 sayings attributed to Jesus. Almost half of these sayings resemble those found in the Canonical Gospels, while the other sayings were previously unknown. Its place of origin may have been Syria, where Thomasine traditions were strong. The introduction states: These are the hidden words that the living Jesus spoke and Didymos Judas Thomas wrote them down. [Didymus (Greek) and Thomas (Aramaic) both mean "twin."] It is possible that the document originated within a school of early Christians, possibly proto-Gnostics. It is important to note that while the Gospel of Thomas does not directly point to Jesus' divinity, it also does not directly contradict it, and therefore neither supports nor contradicts Gnostic beliefs. When asked his identity in the Gospel of Thomas, Jesus usually deflects, ambiguously asking the disciples why they do not see what is right in front of them. This is similar to passages in the Canonical Gospels like John 12:16 and Luke 18:34. The Gospel of Thomas is very different in tone and structure from other New Testament apocrypha and the four Canonical Gospels. Unlike the Canonical Gospels, it is not a narrative account of the life of Jesus; instead, it consists of logia (sayings) attributed to Jesus, sometimes stand-alone, sometimes embedded in short dialogues or parables. The text contains a possible allusion to the death of Jesus, but doesn't mention crucifixion, resurrection, or final judgment; nor does it mention a messianic understanding of Jesus. Since its discovery, many scholars see it as a proof for the existence of the so-called Q source, which might have been very similar in its form as a collection of sayings of Jesus without any accounts of his deeds or his life and death, a so-called "sayings gospel."

Grandmother: See **Unci**, or **Maka**.

Grandfather: Grandfather as used in this book is a spiritual term often used in Native American language to describe a higher source or intelligence of the universe, and usually represents the male portion of what is sometimes referred to in different spiritual traditions as the Godhead. In Native American usage this godhead would be comprised of, but not limited to, Grandfather and Grandmother (see Grandmother, Unci, or Maka). During ritual or prayer Grandfather is usually perceived as existing or permeating the upper part of the environment which includes the sky, sun, or celestial bodies. There is no hierarchy concerning the combined forces of Grandfather or Grandmother, but it is conceived as working together in nature as "the spirit that moves in all things" or a force permeating nature, or the natural world as we see it.

Green Frog Skins: A term coined or made famous by the great Holy Man Lame Deer, meaning money or dollar bills.

Guru: A guru (Sanskrit) is one who is regarded as having great knowledge, wisdom, and authority in a certain area, and who uses it to guide others (teacher). Other forms of manifestation of this principle can include parents, school teachers, non-human objects (books) and even one's own intellectual discipline, if the aforementioned are in a guidance role. In the religious sense the term is commonly used in Hinduism, as well as in other Indian religions and new religious movements. Finding a true guru is often held to be a prerequisite for attaining self-realization. In contemporary India, the word guru is widely used with the general meaning of teacher. In Western usage, the meaning of guru has been extended to cover anyone who acquires followers, though not necessarily in an established school of philosophy or religion.

Hecheto Welo: A Lakota people's term for "It is good."

Hexagram: A hexagram as referred to in this book is part of the
I-Ching's system of divination. It is comprised of six lines which are
obtained by throwing three coins or manipulating Yarrow stalks. The
hexagram is built line by line, either a broken line (Yin) or a solid
line (Yang) until there are six lines or a hexagram. This hexagram
is then looked up in the I-Ching or Book of Changes to determine
where you are, what is happening to you at that particular time, or in
answer to a question you have posed.

Higher self: The higher self is a term used to denote coming from
an area of consciousness that is on a higher spiritual level than the
normal everyday ego-self; so in a sense it is not your "self," but
more of a spiritual essence. It is sometimes referred to as "The Sage,"
"Christ Consciousness," "The Source," and other words trying to
describe what actually can't be described. The closest description may
be "enlightenment."

Hippie: The hippie subculture was originally a youth movement that
arose in the United States during the mid-1960s and spread to other
countries around the world. The etymology of the term "hippie" is
from hipster, and was initially used to describe beatniks who had
moved into San Francisco's Haight-Ashbury district. Both the words
"hip" and "hep" came from African American culture and denote
"awareness." The early hippies inherited the counter cultural values
of the Beat Generation, created their own communities, listened to
psychedelic rock, embraced the sexual revolution, and used drugs
such as cannabis, LSD, and magic mushrooms to explore altered states
of consciousness.

I-Ching: The I-Ching (Wade-Giles) or Yì Jìng (Pinyin), also known as the Classic of Changes, Book of Changes, and Zhouyi, is one of the oldest of the Chinese classic texts. The book contains a divination system comparable to Western geomancy or the West African Ifá system; in Western cultures and modern East Asia, it is still widely used for this purpose. Traditionally, the I-Ching and its hexagrams were thought to pre-date recorded history, and based on traditional Chinese accounts, its origins trace back to between the 3rd and 2nd millennium BC. Modern scholarship suggests that the earliest layer of the text may date from the end of the 2nd millennium BC, but place doubts on much of the mythological aspects in the traditional accounts. Some consider the I-Ching's extant compilation dates back to 1,000 BC. The oldest manuscripts that have been found, albeit incomplete, are texts written on bamboo slips and date to the Warring States Period. During the Warring States Period the text was re-interpreted as a system of cosmology and philosophy that subsequently became intrinsic to Chinese culture. It centered on the ideas of the dynamic balance of opposites, the evolution of events as a process, and acceptance of the inevitability of change.

Joseph Campbell: Joseph John Campbell (March 26, 1904 – October 30, 1987) was an American mythologist, writer and lecturer, best known for his work in comparative mythology and comparative religion. His work is vast, covering many aspects of the human experience. His philosophy is often summarized by his phrase: "Follow your bliss."

Kola: Means "friend" in Lakota.

Kwan Yin: Or Guanyin is the Bodhisattva associated with compassion as venerated by East Asian Buddhists, usually as a female. The name Guanyin is short for Guanshiyin which means "Observing the Sounds (or Cries) of the World." She is also sometimes referred to as Guanyin Pusa. Some Buddhists believe that when one of their adherents departs from this world, they are placed by Guanyin in the heart of a lotus, then sent home to the western pure land of Sukhavati. It is generally accepted (in the Chinese community) that Guanyin originated as the Sanskrit Avalokitesvara, which is her male form. Commonly known in English as the Mercy Goddess or Goddess of Mercy, Guanyin is also revered by Chinese Taoists (sometimes called Daoists) as an Immortal. However, in Taoist mythology, Guanyin has other origination stories which are not directly related to Avalokitesvara.

Lakota: The Lakota, Teton, Tetonwan ("dwellers of the prairie") Sioux are a Native American tribe. They are part of a confederation of seven related Sioux tribes, or seven council fires, and speak Lakota, one of the three major dialects of the Sioux language. The Lakota are the western-most of the three Sioux-language groups, occupying lands in both North and South Dakota. They consist of seven bands or sub-tribes. Notable persons include Sitting Bull from the Hunkpapa band; and Crazy Horse, Red Cloud, Black Elk, Spotted Tail, Billy Mills, and Touch the Clouds from the Oglala band.

Lame Deer: Lame Deer (Lakota 1903–1976), also known as John Fire, John (Fire) Lame Deer, and later, The Old Man, was a Lakota holy man. He belonged to the Heyoka society. Lame Deer was a Mineconju-Lakota Sioux born on the Rosebud Indian Reservation.

His father was Silas Fire Let-Them-Have-Enough. His mother was Sally Red Blanket. He lived and learned with his grandparents until he was 6 or 7, after which he was placed in a day school near the family until age fourteen. He was then sent to a boarding school, one of many run by the U.S. Bureau of Indian Affairs for Indian youth. These schools were designed to "civilize" the Native Americans after their forced settlement on reservations. Lame Deer's life as a young man was rough and wild; he traveled and rode the rodeo circuit as a rider and later as a rodeo clown. According to his personal account, he drank, gambled, womanized, and once went on a several day long car theft and drinking binge. Eventually, he happened upon the house where the original peace pipe given to the Lakota by White Buffalo Calf Woman was kept; much to his surprise, the keeper of the pipe told Lame Deer she had been waiting for him for some time. This served as a turning point in Lame Deer's life. He settled down and began his life as a "wichasa wakan" ("medicine man," or more accurately, "holy man").

Lao Tzu: Laozi, Lao Tzu; also Lao Tse, Lao Tu, Lao-Tzu, Lao-Tsu, Laotze, Laosi, Lao Zi, Laocius, and other variations, was a mystic philosopher of ancient China, best known as the author of the Tao Te Ching (often simply referred to as Laozi). His association with the Tao Te Ching has led him to be traditionally considered the founder of Taoism (pronounced as Daoism). He is also revered as a deity in most religious forms of the Taoist religion, which often refers to Laozi as Taishang Laojun, or "One of the Three Pure Ones." Laozi translated literally from Chinese means "old master" or "old one," and is generally considered honorific. According to Chinese tradition, Laozi lived in the 6th century BCE. Historians variously contend that Laozi is a synthesis of multiple historical figures, that he is a mythical figure, or that he actually lived in the 5th-4th century BCE, concurrent with the Hundred Schools of Thought and Warring States Period. A central figure in Chinese culture, both nobility and common people claim Laozi in their lineage. Throughout history, Laozi's work has been embraced by various anti-authoritarian movements.

Luta: A Lakota people's term for the second cardinal point of the north, one of the four directions. It represents purification, renewal, and rest. It is a place of quiet meditation. The color is red.

Maka: A Lakota people's term for the earth. The "spirit essence" of the feminine energy. This energy is sometimes referred to as Grandmother, or Mother Earth, and is an integral part of creation. Grandmother is thought of as the planet or earth on which we live and would be the Yin part of the concept of the Taoist's view of an actuating force called Yin and Yang. However, Grandmother or the Earth would also display many facets of both Yin and Yang. In Lakota ritual or prayer gifts are often offered to Grandmother in the form of tobacco and other herbs.

Maya: Maya (Sanskrit), in Indian religions, has multiple meanings, usually quoted as "illusion," centered on the fact that we do not experience the environment itself but rather a projection of it, created by us. Maya is the principal deity that manifests, perpetuates, and governs the illusion and dream of duality in the phenomenal Universe.

Meditation: Meditation refers to any form of a family of practices in which practitioners train their minds or self-induce a mode of consciousness to realize benefit. Meditation is generally an inwardly oriented, personal practice, which individuals can do by themselves. Prayer beads or other ritual objects may be used during meditation. Meditation may involve invoking or cultivating a feeling or internal state, such as compassion, or attending to a specific focal point. The term can refer to the state itself, as well as to practices or techniques employed to cultivate the state. There are dozens of specific styles of meditation practice; the word meditation may carry different meanings in different contexts. Meditation has been practiced since antiquity as a component of numerous religious traditions.

Mitakuye Oyasin: A Lakota people's term meaning "all my relations" or "we are all one." This would include all races, and species of animal, the planet and the universal order of things, or "the spirit that moves in all things."

Mushin: Mushin (Japanese mushin; English translation "without mind") is a mental state into which very highly trained martial artists are said to enter during combat. They also practice this mental state during everyday activities. The term is shortened from "mushin no shin," a Zen expression meaning the mind without mind and is also referred to as the state of "no-mindness." That is a mind not fixed or occupied by thought or emotion and thus open to everything.

Nag Hammadi: Nag Hammadi, Egypt, is best known for being the site where local farmers found a sealed earthenware jar containing thirteen leather-bound papyrus codices, together with pages torn from another book, in December 1945. The mother of the farmers burned one of the books and parts of a second (including its cover). Thus twelve of these books (one missing its cover) and the loose pages survive. The writings in these codices, dating back to the 2nd century AD, comprised 52 mostly Gnostic tractates (treatises), believed to be a library hidden by monks from the nearby monastery of St. Pachomius when the possession of such banned writings, denounced as heresy, was made an offense. The contents of the Coptic-bound codices were written in Coptic, though the works were probably all translations from Greek. Most famous of these works must be the Gospel of Thomas, of which the Nag Hammadi codices contain the only complete copy. All the texts have been public since 1975, and are available online.

Nicaea: The First Council of Nicaea was a council of Christian bishops convened in Nicaea in Bithynia (present-day Iznik in Turkey) by the Roman Emperor Constantine I in A.D. 325. The Council was the first effort to attain consensus in the church through an assembly representing all of Christendom. Its main purpose was to settle the Christological issue of the relationship of Jesus to God the Father; the construction of the first part of the Nicene Creed; settling the calculation of the date of Easter; and promulgation of early canon law. Some consider these events as a manipulation of canons or codices for purposes of giving a slanted view of Christological issues.

Okaga Ska: A Lakota people's term for the last and fourth cardinal point of the south and the color white. It is the direction of the spirit world or the world beyond this one.

Pantheon: A pantheon is a set of all the gods of a particular poly-theistic religion or mythology.

Red Road: To walk a sacred path in life giving honor and reverence to yourself, the planet, and all living things. To walk the path of tribal ancestors who were one with the earth.

Sacred Circle: The sacred circle of life in nature or the natural order of things. Everything is a circle with a beginning and an ending in a continuous flow, thus in a sense no beginning and ending. A cyclical event. A sacred circle could also be a tribal or kindred group, such as a circle of friends.

Sage or Sagebrush: Sage is a shrub or small tree from the family Asteraceae. The vernacular name "sagebrush" is also used for several related members of the genus Artemisia, such as California sagebrush. Sage is used in Native American cultures for cleansing negative energies and/or ridding oneself of a bad spirit. It is sometimes mixed with other herbs such as sweet grass and tobacco when smoking the sacred pipe or what some may call a peace pipe.

Sapa: A Lakota people's term for the first cardinal point of the west and one of the spirits of the four directions. It is the direction of the winged ones and the Thunderbeings or Wakinyan. It is represented by the color black.

Sioux: The Sioux are Native American and First Nations people in North America. The term can refer to any ethnic group within the Great Sioux Nation or any of the Nation's many language dialects. The Sioux comprise three major divisions based on Siouan dialect and subculture. The Sioux maintain many separate tribal governments scattered across several reservations, communities, and reserves in the

Dakotas, Nebraska, Minnesota, and Montana in the United States; and Manitoba and southern Saskatchewan in Canada.

Sitting Bull: Sitting Bull (c. 1831 – December 15, 1890) was a Hunkpapa Lakota Sioux holy man who led his people as a tribal chief during years of resistance to United States government policies. Born near the Grand River in Dakota Territory, he was killed by Indian agency police on the Standing Rock Indian Reservation during an attempt to arrest him and prevent him from supporting the Ghost Dance movement. Sitting Bull's premonition of defeating the cavalry at Little Big Horn became reality. At the climactic moment, "Sitting Bull intoned, 'The Great Spirit has given our enemies to us. We are to destroy them.'" Seven months after the battle, Sitting Bull and his group left the United States to Wood Mountain, Saskatchewan, where he remained until 1881, at which time he surrendered to U.S. forces. After his return to the United States, he briefly toured as a performer in Buffalo Bill Cody's Wild West Show, earning $50 a week. During the period 1868–1876, Sitting Bull developed into the most impor-tant of Native American chiefs.

Spirit: The English word "spirit" (from Latin *spiritus*, "breath") has many differing meanings and connotations, most of them relating to a non-corporeal substance contrasted with the material body. The spirit of a living thing usually refers to or explains its consciousness. Spirit is sometimes used to indicate the larger spirit of things, as in the Native American term Great Spirit or Grandfather, Grandmother, and the spirits of the four directions.

Spiritual: Spirituality can refer to an ultimate or an alleged immate-rial reality; an inner path enabling a person to discover the essence of his/her being; or the deepest values and meanings by which people live. Spiritual practices, including meditation, prayer and contemplation, are intended to develop an individual's inner life; spiritual experience includes that of connectedness with a larger reality, yielding a more comprehensive self; with other individuals or the human community; with nature or the cosmos; or with the divine realm. Spirituality is often experienced as a source of inspiration or orientation in life. It can encompass belief in immaterial realities or experiences of the immanent or transcendent nature of the world.

Sufism: Sufism is defined by its adherents as the inner, mystical dimension of Islam. A practitioner of this tradition is generally known as a Sufi. Another name for a Sufi is Dervish. Classical Sufi scholars have defined Sufism as "a science whose objective is the reparation of the heart and turning it away from all else but God. Alternatively, a science through which one can know how to travel into the presence of the Divine, purify one's inner self from filth, and beautify it with a variety of praiseworthy traits."

Sword of No Sword: "The Sword of No Sword" is a term coined by traditional Japanese martial artists and is a concept of using what might be called the sword of the spirit. In a sense it means that even though you might have a physical sword or other weapon (including the hands) and be proficient at the martial arts, you would not use such knowledge or weapons against the opponent physically, but only as a last resort. This could be accomplished in several ways. One way would be by walking away from a situation that was intuitively perceived as dangerous. Another would be to fend off the opponent's energy by driving him away with a projection of chi or spiritual energy. This last technique is sometimes considered the ultimate attainment of martial training. This last technique has been described as a kind of negative proximity factor.

Tao: Tao, or Dao, is a Chinese word meaning way, path, route, or sometimes, more loosely, doctrine or principle.

Taoist: Taoism (also spelled Daoism) refers to a philosophical or religious tradition in which the basic concept is to establish harmony with the Tao, which is everything that exists, the origin of everything; and because of the latter it is also nothing.

Tao Te Ching: The Tao Te Ching, Dao De Jing, or Daodejing, also simply referred to as Laozi, whose authorship has been attributed to Laozi, is a Chinese classic text. Its name comes from the opening words of its two sections. According to tradition, it was written around the 6th century BC by the sage Laozi (or Lao Tzu, "Old Master"), a record-keeper at the Zhou Dynasty court, by whose name the text is known in China. The text's true authorship and date of composition or compilation are still debated, although the oldest excavated text dates back to the late 4th century BC. The text is fundamental to the Philosophical Taoism and strongly influenced other schools, such as Legalism and Neo-Confucianism. This ancient book is also central in Chinese religion, not only for Religious Taoism but Chinese Buddhism, which when first introduced into China was largely interpreted through the use of Taoist words and concepts. Many Chinese artists, including poets, painters, calligraphers, and even gardeners have used the Tao Te Ching as a source of inspiration. Its influence has also spread widely outside East Asia, and is amongst the most translated works in world literature. The

Wade–Giles romanization *Tao Te Ching* dates back to early English transliterations in the late 19th century, and many people continue using it, especially for words and phrases that have become well-established in English. The pinyin romanization *Daodejing* originated in the late 20th century, and this romanization is becoming increasingly popular, having been adopted as the official system by the Chinese government.

The Sage: A sage is any wise teacher, or someone who imparts wisdom or the perennial philosophy. This includes spiritual teachers and teachers of mysticism, but not necessarily with such religious connotations. So "the sage" may refer to a: wise old man, a kind, wise, paternal figure, often archetypal or stereotypical; philosopher, particularly one distinguished for wisdom, depth, or sound judgment; poet, particularly of transcendental or devotional poetry.

Thunderbeings: Thunderbeings are a powerful force of the spirit direction of the west. They represent the force of electrical energy on the earth. They are the force that controls the essence of the clouds, the motion of hurricanes, tornadoes, and storms. Thunderbeings are represented by the Thunderbird called Wakinyan (Lakota). Wakinyan flies without eyes, without ears, without mouth, without nose. Even in visions, no one can behold the Wakinyan whole. Wakinyan is the force of truth and can strike anyone down who lies while holding the sacred pipe. Crazy Horse, the famous Sioux warrior, had a special relationship with the Wakinyan or Thunderbeings. All winged creatures are somehow connected to this awesome force.

Thunderbirds: The Thunderbird is a legendary creature in certain North American indigenous peoples' history and culture. It is considered a supernatural bird of power and strength. It is especially important, and richly depicted, in the art, songs and oral histories of many Pacific Northwest Coast cultures, and is found in various forms among the peoples of the American Southwest and Great Plains. Thunderbirds were major components of the Southeastern Ceremonial Complex of American prehistory. The Thunderbird's name comes from the common belief that the beating of its enormous wings causes thunder and stirs the wind. The Lakota name for the Thunderbird is Wakinyan. The Ojibwa word for a Thunderbird that is closely associated with thunder is Animikii, while large thunderous birds are known as Binesi.

Tom Brown Jr.: Tom Brown Jr. (born January 29, 1950) is an American naturalist, wilderness tracker, and the author of numerous books, including a series of field guides. Brown attributes his tracking skills and his spiritual philosophy to the teachings of a Lipan Apache elder named Stalking Wolf, who instructed Brown during his childhood. Brown refers to Stalking Wolf as "Grandfather" in his writings.

Totem: In modern times, some single individuals, involved or not otherwise involved in the practice of a tribal religion, have chosen to adopt a personal spirit animal helper. This totem has a special meaning to them in a spiritual sense, and will often show up in their life for confirmation of its relationship with them.

Transcendence: In religion, transcendence is a trance-like condition or state of being that surpasses physical existence and in one form is also independent of it. It is typically manifested in prayer, meditation, psychedelics, and paranormal visions. It is affirmed in the concept of the divine in the major religious traditions, and contrasts with the notion of God, or the Absolute, existing exclusively in the physical order, or indistinguishable from it (pantheism). Transcendence can be attributed to the divine not only in its being, but also in its knowledge. Thus, God transcends the universe, but also transcends knowledge (is beyond the grasp of the human mind). Although transcendence is defined as the opposite of immanence, the two are not necessarily mutually exclusive. Some theologians and metaphysicians of the great religious traditions affirm that God, or Brahman, is both within and beyond the universe (pantheism); in it, but not of it; simultaneously pervading it and surpassing it.

Tunkashila: A Lakota people's term for Grandfather, Grandfather's breath, or type of holy wind, smoke, and/or steam.

Unci: A Lakota people's term for Mother Earth or Grandmother.

Vision: Sometimes referred to as having a vision or going on a "vision quest." In the Lakota tradition this is called Hanblecheya or "crying for a dream." The traditional procedure is as follows: A boy or young man at around the age of puberty will isolate himself in a pit for four days and nights on top of a hill without food and water. The site is selected by a Medicine Man or Wichasa Wakan (Holy Man) of the tribe. When the seeker descends from the mountain, an interpretation of his vision is given to him from the Wichasa Wakan so he may understand the meaning. Other visions, both within and outside of tribal communities, may be spontaneous and sometimes reveal the future, a special name, or other significant information.

Wakinyan: See Thunderbeings.

Wichasa Wakan: In the Lakota people's language a Wichasa Wakan is a person of the tribe who is what some might call a medicine man or shaman. But the actual meaning of the word is rendered as Holy Man. This person fulfills many roles, including but not limited to healer, counselor, wisdom keeper, seer, leader of sacred ritual, and sacred pipe carrier.

Wind (Ta'te): In the Native American (Lakota) language, meaning Holy Wind, energy, or a voice from a higher source or higher self. A kind of intuition best described as a knowing from listening in an esoteric sense.

Wizard of Oz: "The Wonderful Wizard of Oz" includes treatments of the modern fairy tale (written by L. Frank Baum and first published in 1900) as an allegory or metaphor for the political, economic and social events of America in the 1890s. Scholars have examined four quite different versions of Oz: the novel of 1900, the Broadway play of 1901, the Hollywood film of 1939, and the numerous follow-up Oz novels written after 1900 by Baum and others. The political interpretations focus on the first three, and emphasize the close relationship between the visual images and the storyline to the political interests of the day. Biographers report that Baum had been a political activist in the 1890s with a special interest in the money question of gold and silver, and the illustrator Denslow was a full-time editorial cartoonist for a major daily newspaper. For the 1901 Broadway production Baum inserted explicit references to prominent political characters such as President Theodore Roosevelt.

Yehoshua: see Yeshua.

Yeshua: Yeshua was a common alternative form of the name Joshua "Yehoshuah" in later books of the Hebrew Bible and among Jews of the Second Temple Period. The name corresponds to the Greek spelling Iesous, from which comes the English spelling Jesus. In English the name Yeshua is extensively used by followers of Messianic Judaism as well as other Christian denominations who wish to use what they consider to be Jesus' Hebrew or Aramaic name.

Yin Yang: In Asian philosophy, the concept of "yin yang," which is often referred to in the West as "yin and yang," is used to describe how polar opposites or seemingly contrary forces are interconnected and interdependent in the natural world, and how they give rise to each other in turn. Opposites thus only exist in relation to each other. The concept lies at the origins of many branches of classical Chinese science and philosophy, as well as being a primary guideline of traditional Chinese medicine, and a central principle of different forms of Chinese martial arts and exercise, such as baguazhang, taijiquan (t'ai chi), and qigong (chi kung) and of I-Ching divination. Many natural dualities: dark and light, female and male, low and high, cold and hot, are thought of as manifestations of yin and yang. Yin yang are not opposing forces (dualities), but complementary opposites that interact within a greater whole, as part of a dynamic system. Everything has both yin and yang aspects as light cannot exist without darkness and vice-versa, but either of these aspects may manifest more strongly in particular objects, and may ebb or flow over time. The concept of yin and yang is often symbolized by various forms of the Taijitu symbol, for which it is probably best known in western cultures. There is a perception (especially in the West) that yin and yang correspond to evil and good. However,

Taoist philosophy generally discounts good/bad distinctions and
other dichotomous moral judgments, in preference to the idea
of balance.

Zen: Zen is a school of Mahayana Buddhism. The word Zen is from
the Japanese pronunciation of the Chinese word Chán, which in turn
is derived from the Sanskrit word dhyana, which can be approxi-
mately translated as "meditation" or "meditative state."

Zeus: In the ancient Greek religion, Zeus is the father of gods and
men who ruled the Olympians of Mount Olympus as a father ruled
the family. He is the god of sky and thunder in Greek mythology.
His Roman counterpart is Jupiter.

About the Author

THUNDERHANDS is an accomplished writer, artist, and musician (Native American flute and percussion). But if words can define a person, the following should suffice: In his lifetime, he has done many things. As a musician he has two CDs featuring his flute playing, which comes to him through channeling what he calls "the holy wind." In the martial arts his advanced practice and study includes three major disciplines. In the field of aviation he obtained his private, commercial, and instrument ratings as a pilot, with multi-engine and flight instructor qualifications. He learned tracking as a boy, and has an established oneness with nature. His spiritual knowledge includes life-long study and personal experience with many shamanistic and esoteric practices, as well as spiritual and tribal ritual. He is a practitioner of kriya yoga, kundalini yoga, tantrika, and Chinese inner alchemy. He received his training in acupressure, but uses several modalities for healing. He is well versed on the Biblical teachings of Yeshua, or Jesus, but considers himself spiritual, not religious. And last but not least, he has done an exhaustive study and been an activist for North American native tribes and causes. His own roots are of Métis descent, and his spirituality is universal.

Additional Information and Products

Music CDs and Books by Thunderhands

Books

Listen to the Wind Speak from the Heart

Emergence

CDs

Desert Spirits — Native American Flute & percussion

Tribal Unity — Native American Flute & Percussion

Available at Amazon as mp3 downloads / Thunderhands

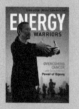

YEAR ZERO: *Time of the Great Shift*

by Kiara Windrider

"I can barely contain myself as I implode with gratitude for the gift of *Year Zero*! Every word resonates on a cellular level, awakening ancient memories and realigning my consciousness with an unshakable knowing that the best has yet to come. This is more than a book; it is a manual for building the new world!"

— Mikki Willis, founder, ELEVATE

ILAHINOOR: *Awakening the Divine Human*

by Kiara Windrider

"Ilahinoor is a truly precious and powerful gift for those yearning to receive and integrate Kiara Windrider's guidance on their journey for spiritual awakening and wisdom surrounding the planet's shifting process."

— Alexandra Delis-Abrams, Ph.D., author *Attitudes, Beliefs, and Choices*

THE MESSAGE: *A Guide to Being Human*

by LD Thompson

"Simple, profound, and moving! The author has been given a gift... a beautiful way to distill the essence of life into an easy-to-read set of truths, with wonderful examples along the way. Listen... for that is how it all starts."

— Lee Carroll, author, the *Kryon* series; co-author, *The Indigo Children*

SOPHIA—THE FEMININE FACE OF GOD:
Nine Heart Paths to Healing and Abundance

by Karen Speerstra

"Karen Speerstra shows us most compellingly that when we open our hearts, we discover the wisdom of the Feminine all around us. A totally refreshing exploration, and beautifully researched read."

— Michael Cecil, author, *Living at the Heart of Creation*

A FULLER VIEW: *Buckminster Fuller's Vision of Hope and Abundance for All*

by L. Steven Sieden

"This book elucidates Buckminster Fuller's thinking, honors his spirit, and creates an enthusiasm for continuing his work."

— Marianne Williamson, author, *Return To Love* and *Healing the Soul of America*

GAIA CALLS: *South Sea Voices, Dolphins, Sharks & Rainforests*

by Wade Daok

"Wade has the soul of a dolphin, and has spent a life on and under the oceans on a quest for deep knowledge. This is an important book that will change our views of the ocean and our human purpose."

— Ric O'Barry, author, *Behind the Dolphin Smile* and star of *The Cove,* which won the 2010 Academy Award for Best Documentary

1.800.833.5738 • 25% discount available online • www.divineartsmedia.com

DIVINE
ARTS

DIVINE ARTS sprang to life fully formed as an intention to bring spiritual practice into daily living. Human beings are far more than the one-dimensional creatures perceived by most of humanity and held static in consensus reality. There is a deep and vast body of knowledge — both ancient and emerging — that informs and gives us the understanding, through direct experience, that we are magnificent creatures occupying many dimensions with untold powers and connectedness to all that is. Divine Arts books and films explore these realms, powers and teachings through inspiring, informative and empowering works by pioneers, artists and great teachers from all the wisdom traditions.

We invite your participation and look forward to learning how we may better serve you.

Onward and upward,

Michael Wiese
Publisher/Filmmaker

DivineArtsMedia.com